ADRIFT *on the* ARK

ADRIFT *on the* ARK
Our Connection to the Natural World

MARGARET THOMPSON

BRINDLE
& GLASS

Library and Archives Canada Cataloguing in Publication
Thompson, Margaret, 1940 Nov. 5–
Adrift on the ark : our connection to the natural world / Margaret Thompson.

ISBN 978-1-897142-41-7

1. Human–animal relationships. 2. Nature—Effect of human beings on.
3. Animals. 4. Thompson, Margaret, 1940 Nov. 5–. I. Title.

QL791.T46 2009   304.2   C2009-902912-X

Editor: Marlyn Horsdal
Cover image: Pete Kohut, incorporating background peacock image by Daniel Andres Forero

 Canada Council   Conseil des Arts
for the Arts   du Canada   Canadian   Patrimoine   BRITISH COLUMBIA
Heritage   canadien   ARTS COUNCIL

Brindle & Glass acknowledges the financial support to its publishing program from the Government of Canada through the Book Publishing Industry Development Program (BPIDP), the Canada Council for the Arts, and the province of British Columbia through the British Columbia Arts Council and Book Publishing Tax Credit.

 Mixed Sources
Product group from well-managed forests, controlled sources and recycled wood or fiber
www.fsc.org Cert no. SW-COC-000952
© 1996 Forest Stewardship Council
FSC
 98%

The interior pages of this book have been printed on 100% post-consumer recycled paper, processed chlorine free, and printed with vegetable-based inks.

Brindle & Glass Publishing
www.brindleandglass.com

1 2 3 4 5 12 11 10 09

PRINTED AND BOUND IN CANADA

For Zachary, Grace, Astrid, and Kurt, because they,
with all the other children, shall inherit the earth.

"This earth is the honey of all beings; all beings the honey of this earth."

    🍃 Upanishads: Famous Debates in the Forest V

"The goal of life is living in agreement with nature."

    🍃 Zeno: Diogenes Laertius;
    Lives of Eminent Philosophers

"In all things of nature, there is something of the marvellous."

    🍃 Aristotle: *Parts of Animals*

CONTENTS

INTRODUCTION

> "But ask now the beasts, and they shall
> teach thee; and the fowls of the air, and
> they shall tell thee."
>
> Job XXI, vii

On this, the first truly hot day of summer, I sit in the shade at the bottom of my garden, doing nothing. The traffic on the nearby highway into Victoria hums along out of sight, a constant undertone, easily ignored. A faint breeze stirs the bamboo along the fence, and a bee fumbles each bell of the white foxglove in turn.

Cedar branches enfold me, drooping fans that filter the sunlight and lace the ground with shifting shadow. Ten feet away, a peahen with a single chick crackles through dry chestnut leaves, prodding for seeds and insects. Every now and then she pauses in her search and tilts her head on one side to point a single watchful eye at the eagles; they are riding the thermals far above the fields where the farmer's clanking tractor chews through the hay, evicting whole families of rodents.

Just above my head, a sturdy branching limb of the cedar supports a robin's nest, empty now, though robins with beakfuls of looped, wavering worms are still a common sight. In the shade of the garden shed, a small black rabbit lies full length, looking like a discarded fur glove. He is safe enough for now; our two basset hounds, usually only too pleased to sit as close to me as possible, and hardwired to chase rabbits, have deserted me for the greater comfort of the kitchen floor tiles. Two gardens away, a neighbour's horse whickers softly, a gentle, companionable sound.

It is almost noon, and the heat is soporific. My eyelids droop, my hand is limp on the page, and my breath slows, but even as this trance-like state deepens, I can hear the minute scratchings of insects, the purr of wings and the rustle as some small creature brushes against a dry leaf, and the dimmest recesses of my brain still discern the ceaseless motion above and below ground, in the air, in light and dark, heat and cold, so beautiful and intricate. I am aware of them all. The Ark has a full complement of passengers relying on us, and awareness is everything.

The ark that is this world, and all its occupants, is sailing troubled seas. The ordinary passenger might be forgiven for throwing up his hands and thinking it is all too late, too far gone, whatever we do is doomed to failure, and what could an individual achieve, anyway? But as the uniquely clever architects of disaster, shouldn't we do whatever is in our power to fix the ship? Even the smallest finger can stop a tiny leak. Noah's story, after all, is about stewardship, about retrieving something from an Earth filled with corruption and violence that seems intent on self-destruction, about hope and survival.

This book is my small contribution to the rescue effort. It grew from my conviction that if only people could feel how indissolubly we are connected to all other living things, how much animals can teach us about co-existence, about restraint, about moderation and balance, we would have to see ourselves in a different light and question our impulse toward disaster.

Very early in my reading life, I came upon my model. When I discovered T.H. White's *The Once and Future King*, I also found his translation of a twelfth-century bestiary, *The Book of Beasts*. Mankind has always been interested in the creatures that share this world, and from the earliest times has told stories and drawn pictures of them. The mythologies of Asia, Ancient Greece, and Egypt are full of animals, some divine, some the servants or companions of the gods, and some hybrids treading strange paths between species, between reality and fantasy. This tradition was succeeded by observers of the world such as Herodotus, Aristotle, Pliny, Solinus, and Aelian. An anonymous person nicknamed The Physiologus cropped up some time between the second and fifth centuries, probably in Egypt, and wrote a book about beasts, possibly in Greek. Whatever the provenance, the book was immensely popular; it was translated into innumerable languages over many centuries, the last handwritten copy having been made in Iceland in 1742. The illuminated bestiaries of the twelfth century in England were the direct descendants of The Physiologus's book, and my starting point.

The bestiaries, with their extraordinary illustrations and even more startling descriptions of the habits of mammals, reptiles, birds, and fish, seem quaint to a modern reader—examples of the dotty beliefs of an ignorant, unscientific age, no more than charming eccentricities.

Within the limitations of their time, however, the bestiaries were the work of serious amateur naturalists, pioneers in the study of biology. There may have been a scrapbook quality about the descriptions, with absolutely no claim to scientific taxonomy, but their authors depended on close and sympathetic observation, even if they were compelled to rely on travellers' tales for details of some of the more exotic animals.

As the product of the Middle Ages—the Age of Faith—they also reflect the love of symbolism and the search for patterns and parallels that distinguish the medieval mindset. Their authors dwelt on the similarities between beasts and man, and stressed the symbolic qualities and spiritual significance of the animals.

Adrift on the Ark is an attempt to carry on this tradition in a way that has some meaning in the secular twenty-first century. The essays deal with animals I have encountered; they are personal, individual "takes" on the interactions between beasts and humans. They are not in any sense a scientific study, not parables, not allegories. I have tried to describe the animals as accurately as possible and unsentimentally, to allow their stories to suggest the larger issues of our co-existence on the planet. In my mind, this is a bestiary for a confused modern world.

IN THE BEGINNING

At least once a year during my childhood, I would wander alone through Eden.

For the most part, those years in England just after the Second World War are uniformly grey in memory. Streets were pockmarked with craters and crumbled masonry, the bombsites barely softened by goldenrod and rose bay willow herb. Air polluted by centuries of coal fires had laid a clammy film of dirt over everything; stone and brick turned black; trains and stations reeked of sulphur. Rationing still prevailed. Apologetically, butchers slid strange offerings into their half-empty windows between the familiar gristly sausages and bony scrag end: I remember dark purple slabs of whale meat; rubbery white tripe; long-hung, blackened hares with bulging, sightless eyes. My clothes were always made several sizes too large, always let out, and let down, as often as not handed down by an older relative, or constructed from the useable portions of a worn-out adult garment.

I never felt deprived. It was the same for everyone, after all, and at seven or eight years old, what would I have had to compare it to? But the pinched, anxious flavour of the time permeated every aspect of life in the faceless, blameless suburb where I lived, first in a small flat over a dress shop, and later in a house beside one of the busiest roads leading southwest out of London.

This depressing miasma rose from the row after row of identical small houses, from the ubiquitous brown paint and varnished interior doors, from the utility furniture, and the smell of boiling cabbage. It hung over the meters which ate sixpences and doled out small portions of gas and electricity to heat rooms and water; over the queues of shoppers lining up, coupon books at the ready, when they heard of a special consignment of woollen vests or butter; over the polar winter bedrooms, where layers of blankets did little to warm the glacial sheets, and the hot-water bottles in their hand-knit covers served only to waken my chilblains to itchy malevolence.

I think I learned very early that the suburbs lacked something essential. Not that I ever articulated such a notion or even consciously entertained the thought. I arrived at it in reverse, by coming to appreciate every opportunity, however meagre, to experience places that were *not* built up, where traffic did *not* thunder by, where there were trees and open spaces and flowers that grew where they wanted rather than where some gardener decided they should, where birds and animals lived mysteriously and moved freely. Such places could exist as little pockets in the middle of suburbia: the towpaths along the Thames, for instance, home to swans and ducks, coots and moorhens; tiny parks that had once been the gardens of private houses; little country lanes that had been cut off, like ox-bow lakes, from the rest of the world when new highways slashed straight across country, leaving the tiny farmyards along them to slumber peacefully in rural backwaters not a quarter of a mile from a main train station.

There were also the places within easy reach of my home that existed because of an untypically far-sighted decision to establish and maintain a Green Belt around London. Thanks to that, I spent many weekends out on the South Downs, roaming the race course at Epsom, listening to the skylarks climb their ladders of song, and toiling to the very top of Box Hill or plunging into the bluebells and the groves of silver birch in the sandy woods of Oxshott.

What these places all had in common was their wildness. A very domestic wildness, to be sure; none of the majestic solitude and awesome grandeur of the Rockies, the Pacific coast, the Antarctic, the Great Rift Valley, the Australian outback. Not *wilderness*. But a place where it was possible to slip away and be quite alone, where the loudest sound might be the hum of bees in a patch of clover, where the wind carried no scent of gasoline or cigarette smoke or drains, where rabbits scurried between burrows, and my long-sighted, country-born father would point out hawks and pheasants, and tell me the names of birds I'd never heard before—dunnock and blue tit, wren and chaffinch, jackdaw and, in the fall, the jewelled goldfinch feasting in chattering flocks on the plumed seeds of giant thistles.

These occasional expeditions served to demonstrate that there was another world beyond the endless houses and pubs and shops and light industry of suburbia, one which offered humans a different connection to their surroundings, no longer as creatures moving about a fabricated landscape, servants always to the mechanisms, systems, and infrastructure of urban settings, but as one among many living entities in a far older, more harmonious environment.

What I knew at the time was that going into the country was special. And that it would be even better to be able to live there all the time.

Fortunately for me, I had relatives who lived in darkest Cambridgeshire and Norfolk, and we visited them every summer. When I was very young, we stayed with my grandmother, who lived with Grandpa in a cottage at the edge of a wheat field. Later, we stayed with my aunt who had a very grand house in the town of Wisbech, where her husband was a pork butcher. That house, which was called The Chestnuts for the massive trees that lined its driveway, was surrounded by acres of land: two orchards, home to dozens of free range hens, a fearsome cockerel which once chased me to everyone's amusement, and sundry ducks which used to swim in superannuated tractor tires; a lovely flower garden surrounded by a rose-covered walkway; and a huge vegetable garden, with peas and scarlet runners, great beds of strawberries, graves of potatoes, raspberry canes (which I ransacked, cramming berries warm from the sun into my mouth), gooseberries, white, red, and black currants, Victoria plum trees beloved of the wasps and my aunt, a long raised bed of asparagus fern (I never once ate any asparagus from this crop, but the ferns were useful in flower arrangements), and two rows of sweet peas, constantly picked to fill the house with scent all summer long.

There was never any of the pinched anxiety in this world. Accustomed to abundance, my aunts gently mocked my mother for spreading butter on bread and then scraping most of it off. All you had to do to get an egg was to feel around underneath a warm hen in the coop. My uncle was a butcher; there was always meat on the table, and most of it would have come from his own farm. My memories of those holidays are full of sun and space: the fields of black loam stretching to the flat horizon under vast cloudscapes; sunflowers and hollyhocks nodding over garden walls; the scent of roses and sweet peas heavy on the air as I played and browsed in the garden, stroked the black or golden Labrador retriever—there was always at least one in residence—and made a friend of my aunt's little corgi, whose name, imaginatively, was Corgi, and whose abused puppy-hood before my aunt rescued him from the stable where he was born had left him fearful of human touch and mortally afraid of children. I collected eggs and carried pails of food to the hens, scratched my uncle's pigs behind the ear and fearlessly stroked the velvet noses of his massive Suffolk Punch draft horses while my mother cringed and shuddered. Half of me belonged to this world, I felt fiercely, and somehow it was the better half.

But these visits, paradisiacal though they were, were just a warm-up for the real thing. Once again, my father provided the key. He worked for a small wholesale seed firm and one of his tasks was to visit the head gardener at Buscot Park in Berkshire on business. Since he elected to make these journeys on Saturdays, my mother and I went with him, and so I found my way into Eden.

On the face of it, it was just a typical estate of the landed gentry, close to a small village called Faringdon. The Queen Anne house nestled at the heart of immaculate lawns and dovecotes, formal flower gardens and kitchen gardens with walls of rosy old brick, greenhouses full of exotic flowers and grapevines, an orangery, two lakes, fields where cattle grazed and a mixed forest filled with great beech trees. This was the country home of that most English of oxymorons, a Socialist peer called Lord Faringdon, and enclosed, as Paradise should be, by a stone wall that snaked its way round the perimeter for miles, interrupted every now and then by large, wrought-iron gates, firmly closed.

The head gardener, Mr. Chapman, lived in a stone cottage on the grounds. He and my father would quickly disappear into the nearest greenhouse; my mother would gossip with Mrs. Chapman; I walked straight through their kitchen, over the slate floor, out the back door and into the woods. Until tea time, I was free.

I don't remember ever telling anyone what I did or what I saw on those golden afternoons. Maybe I understood intuitively that my experiences would not bear translation; they were deeply felt, though, and profoundly influential.

I would abandon myself to the space, wandering through the beech woods past the badger sett, up to the summer house overlooking the wilder of the two lakes—a reservoir actually, I believe—a dimpled body of grey water rimmed with stiff sedge, with moorhens darting in and out of its cover. I would find white peacock feathers and hear their owners' distant cries. I would follow a neglected man-made watercourse that slipped down the hill over steps green with algae, past an abandoned tennis court, its net looped over a rotting post, down to the other lake. There I would watch a squadron of Canada geese sculling about on the water round an island covered with tall trees. Large untidy nests filled the treetops; herons constantly came and went, blundering about in the branches, wings flapping like parasols in a high wind as they came in to land. On the bank I once found a dead mole, a little grey velvet purse, its blind snout and pink hands unbearably affecting. I watched a fox slowly backing into the lake, submerging until only the tip of his nose showed above the surface, and then even that disappeared. This, I later discovered, was probably to rid himself of fleas, but the animal's careful stealth seemed momentous, like some mysterious rite of passage. Just as stirring was the snake that slid away from my foot, poured itself without a pause into the stream and swam away like quicksilver, the elegant curves of its passage propelling the tiny pointed head.

When his lordship was away, I would circle back up to the house. I had no interest in the building, never wanted to get inside, and indeed, on the one occasion I was allowed to view the interior, found it uninteresting except for the paintings on the bathroom wall. Instead, I would stand on the lawn and watch the white fantail pigeons. With chests absurdly inflated, like spinnakers, tails erect and unfurled, wings drooping just a little, and cooing throatily, the males wheeled to and fro, round and round about the females, who ignored them with studied indifference. Their courtship amused me—such histrionics, such teasing!—but it wasn't until much later, when I had attended recitals featuring eminent tenors in full evening dress pouring adoration or recrimination from the depths of their massive barrel chests, that I saw the pigeons' display for the theatrical performance it really was.

Those infrequent visits were revelatory. At the time, I simply gloried in the freedom from adult supervision, hugging to myself all I saw and heard as something uniquely mine. The memories of those times are always with me; I have come back to them over and over again in my life. Obviously, there is more to them than the solitary pleasures of an introspective child.

That I was alone is important; that I was solitary and not lonely is more so. I think that distant child divined that she lived in a world of wonders, none of her making; that she lived alongside creatures no less important than she, and no more, whose ways were mysterious and profoundly right; that she had a place in this world, but only if she left those creatures to go about their business, just as they were inclined to leave her to hers; that the happiness she felt in their company came from balance, from respect, from love.

I came very early, then, to an awareness that we have much to learn from the animals around us. Hindsight tells me that I was probably born too late; I would have made a good naturalist of the kind that flourished in the nineteenth century, pursuing a passion for songbirds, or snails in one particular valley, writing erudite little monographs, becoming an authority . . . Reality in the shape of an apparent total blind spot where mathematics was concerned, which led to the dubious distinction of my being the only girl in my year at school *not* to take GCE Ordinary Level Maths, brought the door to a science degree crashing shut and I went another way. But I have never lost my passion for the living world, and my fascination with its occupants, nor my consciousness of the myriad lives that whirl about and intersect with my own.

This passion makes me a tiresome companion, I admit. When I am supposed to be concentrating on a conversation, my eye will be caught by a movement, and before I know it I am blurting out, "Oh, look—a pileated woodpecker!" or worse, abruptly coming to a halt while driving to watch a group of baby raccoons by the side of the road. If I am a bit obsessive, though, it is because I have proved many times to my own satisfaction that such passionate awareness of nature is a comfort, a reminder—in all the wreckage of human relations—of harmony and stability, the way things ought to be.

In my lifetime, it seems, humankind has pushed that delicate equilibrium far out of balance. Ignorance may account for the crimes of the past: the mass slaughter of the inoffensive dodo, for example, unafraid of humans, meekly allowing itself to be hit over the head; or the sterility of pelicans, and other birds worldwide, because of the overuse of DDT. We cannot claim ignorance now; we are bombarded with information.

Yet a kind of wilful ignorance prevails. Self-preservation, one would think, would incline us to do as little as possible to render our environment uninhabitable, yet greed and desperate need embrace short-sighted decisions. So the rainforest burns and the glaciers retreat while ever more people turn their backs on the land and crowd into our sprawling, teeming cities as fast as they can.

In the beginning, the old story tells us, the lion lay down with the lamb. Such forbearance is the stuff of fantasy, of course—were the lions vegetarians then?—but the image is a reminder of how far we humans have strayed from the ideal. Unless peaceful co-existence, harmony and moderation become our reality, we shall never see Eden again.

PETS Я US

Heavy snowfalls and cold, and the attendant privations suffered by wildlife, show just how many animals live close to us. We are, in fact, surrounded by them, hemmed in on all sides by non-human creatures, even in the cities.

Just along our short cul-de-sac in Greater Victoria rove dozens of every size and shape: thirteen peacocks; an indefinite and fluctuating number of plump grey and black rabbits; several peripatetic deer; a covey of California quail; a pair of Northern Flickers; and the usual concentrations of small songbirds—juncos, sparrows, chickadees, nuthatches and brown creepers, wrens, towhees, Anna's hummingbirds and the like. Near neighbours keep goats and turkeys; the valley we overlook is home to many horses and riding stables; cows, like nursery figures, dot the distant fields. At certain times of the year, on a variable schedule known only to them, hundreds of trumpeter swans populate those same fields and ride the air past my windows, bright white against the overcast.

We try hard to help them all in the occasional extreme weather. After our last storm, several local residents joined me in feeding the peacocks. My neighbour mounted a near-Polar expedition in appalling road conditions to bring home a good supply of hay for her horses. Some people came up with ingenious devices to warm the hummingbird feeders.

These efforts were all basically altruistic: nobody expects gratitude. Peacocks will line up for more but they never write thank you notes, and if you presume on that acquaintance and try to touch one, it will certainly turn on the hand that feeds it. The only time we ever form what may be called a relationship with animals is when we domesticate them. Even then, the relationship is one-sided. Having your need for food and shelter taken care of in return for supplying food or service to humans does not involve the warmth and mutual pleasure that the word "relationship" implies. Only those privileged creatures we admit to our homes, our furniture, and our hearts get anything more than subsistence out of their connection to humans. Pets are a breed apart.

When you come right down to it, keeping a pet is a very strange business. For some people, of course, it is quite straightforward. They are the ones who would describe themselves without a qualm as owners, as masters (and mistresses). They would have no patience with politically correct labels such as "caregiver" or "companion," and would be completely unmoved by the ghostly reminders of slavery, and of archaic laws concerning goods and chattels, inherent in the idea of owning a living creature.

These are not thoughts that ever occur to most people embarking on a search for the perfect family pet. There may be, in the case of dogs and cats, a vague notion that the animal could have its uses; cats will keep vermin at bay, for instance, or dogs will guard the home or its occupants. Most of the cats I've known are far too well fed to take up hunting seriously. As for dogs, they will certainly bark if they hear an intruder, but judging by mine, would overwhelm the burglar with the rapture of their welcome rather than put him to flight.

The reality is that with a pet, you take on an added dependant, one you have to supply with food, shelter, security, companionship, education, entertainment, grooming, medical and dental care—even, possibly, insurance—for as long as the animal lives. Love is a desirable extra for the animal. Essentially, it is the same as adopting a child.

And it comes with the same risks. An adopted baby is a surprise package. The adoptive parents may know something of the child's background, but that will not necessarily prepare them for genetic disorders or fetal alcohol syndrome. A person seeking a pet is in the same position. The breeder may be able to supply proof that the puppy or kitten has the blood of champions, but that is no guarantee of perfect health, and there is even less certainty that the cute puppy at the pet store will not be deaf, or suffer hip dysplasia, or inexplicably take chunks out of the postman.

We once adopted a most beautiful springer spaniel called Tally, a loving, bustling dog full of vibrant energy, boasting a pedigree loaded with champions. He was also quite mad. He would bark himself hoarse at tree roots and empty paper bags, and obsessively pursue bicycle wheels and men in shorts. When I had apologetically applied first aid to a number of cyclists who had ended up in the ditch outside our house, and Tally one day expanded his concept of the enemy to include women with small children in strollers, we had to part company. It was not a hard decision, but a difficult thing to do.

So why do so many of us take on these liabilities so willingly? Why do we put up with the mud they track into our houses, the hairs and feathers they shed, the things they chew to pieces, the trouble they can cause?

To find answers to these questions I have only to look at some of the dogs I have lived with. This is not to discount cats, or parrots, or ferrets or guinea pigs, or any of the other creatures people call pets. Rather, making dogs the exemplar is a recognition that "man's best friend" is more than a cliché, and may offer the easiest access to some profound truths about animals.

The first of these truths is that after living with a dog, nobody could ever deny that animals are sentient individuals. Just like human beings, they have personality. Just like us, they feel love and joy, despair and grief, curiosity and pain. Just like us, they have memories, and they experience hope and resignation.

My husband, Alan, and I share our house with two basset hounds called William and Lucy. Being the same breed, they are alike in appearance: black, white, and tan fur, long bodies, short legs, enormous feet, dangling velvety ears, stiff tails held jauntily like banners, and soulful faces. Both are friendly and very stubborn, both love to sleep on the couch, both hate water and walk around puddles if they possibly can, both will eat anything at any time no matter how vile, both are essentially noses on four legs, and both were adopted from Basset Rescues.

Other than that, they could not be more different.

William is very laid-back. He spends a good part of his life sleeping and lying in the sun (when available); he enjoys a walk, but is quite likely to stop dead when he's had enough and refuse to go farther unless you turn around, when he will triumphantly lead the way back to the car. He firmly believes that everyone he sees has come by especially to visit him, so he tends to approach perfect strangers unloading things from their trucks, or wait for people crossing from the other side of the road, barking and waving his tail in greeting. His trust is so transparently guileless, like that of a three-year-old child, that this ploy invariably works. People everywhere stop to speak to him and fondle his ears.

This trust is amazing given his experiences in the eighteen months before he came to live with us. The rescue people told us that he grew up in Prince Rupert, was kept outside all the time, ignored, never housetrained, and then institutionalized, going to four other foster homes in the Lower Mainland before we heard about him.

This early history was substantiated in the most remarkable way. We were sitting outside a local café, talking with another dog owner who happened to mention that he had once managed the theatre in Prince Rupert. Just to contribute to the conversation, we revealed that William had come from the same city, and described his first home.

As we related this, a strange inward look came over the man's face.

"I *know* that place," he said. "I used to walk past it every day on the way to work. I'd stop and talk to the dog through the fence. And one day I sneaked around the back of the house to see if he had any shelter, and he didn't, so I phoned the SPCA."

We are grateful for his intervention. William's early life has left its scars: despite great progress in the housetraining department, he still has accidents; loneliness probably made him bark incessantly, and somebody found a vet prepared to debark him, leaving him with a muffled, high-pitched girly bark and a falsetto bay. Most pathetically, he never learned how to play and now seems at such a loss, when faced with another dog who is ready to gambol, that he can only resort to barking wildly.

He is a strikingly handsome dog, unusually dark, with a noble domed head which owes much to his bloodhound connections. His coat is silken and the loose skin about his head and neck invites the hand irresistibly into its plush folds. A lady seeing him walk into Butchart Gardens one day cried out, "Oh, aren't you just a comfortable old shoe!" And he is the most endearing mix of elder statesman and clown, sitting with his Queen Anne legs turned out in classic first position as if he has attended ballet classes, and a baffled expression on his face.

You have only to look into his eyes, to feel his weight leaning into your leg, to watch his eyebrows twitch from side to side as he lays his head on his paws and watches your every move, to know that he is capable of the deepest affection—devotion, even—and loyalty.

Lucy is loving, too, but completely different in personality. She came to us at a year old from the Western Washington Basset Rescue, by way of eastern Washington and Utah. She had been abandoned, and possibly abused. When we first met her, she was a gangly teenager who looked more like a large beagle than a basset hound, but she has matured into a lovely dog with melting eyes and a dusting of light brown freckles over her white nose.

She is a busy dog. I put it down to a very active mind; she is endlessly curious about everything. At first, despite the rescue lady's somewhat hesitant reassurance—"I *think* she's over the chewing stage now"—this manifested itself in a destructive rampage of dismembered books, torn slippers, splintered plastic pens, CDs, DVDs and their jewel cases, razors, toothbrushes, brooms and dustpans, ripped-up towels, facecloths, gloves and socks, disembowelled stuffed toys, cushions and quilts, gnawed sticks from the garden, and, in the spirit of not letting a similar captive resource go to waste, gnawed chair legs, ottoman bases, and several wicker baskets. She even tore a strip of lino off the kitchen floor.

She still crunches the occasional matchbox or sheet of bubble wrap, but it is a game now rather than an obsession, for she is very playful. Now she steals socks for the sheer pleasure of darting off with them, twitching them just out of reach as you try to retrieve them. For a while, though, she nearly drove us mad, and our basement had to be dog-proofed, just as you would remove everything from the lower four feet of a room in order to safeguard an experimental toddler bent on sticking his fingers into the electrical outlets and climbing the bookshelves.

Naturally, she regards William as a dead loss where games are concerned and leaves him in no doubt as to who is in charge. Intellectually, she runs rings around William and is capable of the most sophisticated manipulation. We have often observed her giving the oblivious William the evil eye as he lolls on her favourite bed, following this up a little later with a convincing display of alarm—a sudden dash through the dog door, barking loudly. William always falls for it. He rears up out of sleep, snorting, and scrambles outside. We will hear his soprano bay ring out at the bottom of the garden over and over, while Lucy crashes back through the dog door and nips smartly onto his still-warm spot on the couch.

Lucy leads the way on walks. William trots behind, content to let her nose out the choicest smells. Not surprisingly, she is far more vocal than

William; she has a massive bark that would make you think you had a bull mastiff to deal with if you heard it on the other side of a closed door, but she also has a large repertoire of small sounds—yips and whines, sighs and grunts and groans. Sometimes she barks directly at us, mostly when we are more than usually dense about interpreting her needs. We may be a bit thick, but there is no doubt that she communicates.

Yet this exuberant, confident dog has her phobias. When we first knew her, we saw how she cowered if anyone raised an arm suddenly, or if she had to pass a man carrying a large solid object such as a briefcase or a guitar, and how she skulked out of her way, dragging us with her, to avoid strollers, wheelchairs, shopping carts, and horses.

It is a commonplace to claim that one's pet has personality, but it is a critically important insight. If all children see that animals are individuals who experience emotions that parallel their own, perhaps we shall one day produce a generation that could no more imagine tethering a dog outside without food or water or shelter, or abandoning a horse in deep snow on a mountainside, than they would their siblings or their best friends.

Such treatment is only possible when the victims are seen as things. If farmers gave all their steers names, beef would probably be a relatively rare commodity. This holds true for human beings, too. It was no accident that the Nazis in their propaganda equated Jews with vermin, and the Hutus referred to Tutsis as cockroaches. However, once the creature, whatever it may be, is seen as an individual, all mistreatment stands revealed as the gross betrayal and abandonment of responsibility and morality that it is.

Because our pets always keep their end of the bargain. Whatever they receive in the way of food, shelter, and contact, they return in the form of devotion and loyalty.

William and Lucy make us laugh and keep us moving. They forgive us when we duck out of taking them for a walk if it's pouring with rain (their dislike of water helps, too). Their pleasures are very simple, almost ascetic; an occasional meaty bone is ecstasy. They are always welcoming and happy to see us. They bear no grudges. They comfort us with their touch and the warmth of their bodies. They have the occasional fierce disagreement but the ensuing snarls and clacking of teeth are forgotten in five minutes; for the most part, they are models of peaceful co-existence. If we pay attention, they teach us how to live.

And how to die.

By and large, humans live much longer than most of the animals we keep as pets. Almost inevitably, anyone with a pet observes that animal for its entire lifespan and thus, every pet offers a course in mortality. That is important for creatures who can imagine their own demise and recognize its inevitability, but knowing about getting old or sick is nothing compared to handling the process well.

Humans tend to whine and complain, some more than others. We fear pain and disability and dependence. Death is unknowable and has ten thousand separate doors, and we fear that, too. Animals have a lot to teach us about acceptance.

We once had a sweet-natured Dalmatian called Tuppence. As we discovered on her very first visit to the vet as a small puppy, she was stone deaf, but she compensated for that by focusing intently on us whenever we were in her line of sight. She was a much loved member of the family, even if she did tend to push us out of bed by lying between us, bracing her back against one of us and stretching her legs against the other.

Later in her life she started to have seizures. At first they were brief, but gradually they became more and more frequent, and were of greater and greater intensity. She would lose control of her bladder as she shuddered and twitched, and would drool helplessly. In her last weeks, each seizure lasted almost an hour and left her limp and confused for days. There was no cure for her, and her life was beginning to consist of lying around trying to recover before the next seizure felled her. We played God, as humans do with animals although they shrink from doing the same to their own kind. We decided we had to end her suffering.

Anyone who watches an animal suffer is struck by its dignity. Small injuries they ignore or tend to themselves. If they feel under the weather they do not make everyone else's life miserable, but quietly sleep until they recover. Chronic pain silences them; they are stoics. They do not bore anyone who will listen with details of their symptoms or blow-by-blow accounts of their surgeries. They do not curse their doctors or shout at their nurses. They never rail against Fate and moan, "Why me?" Despite her desperate condition, Tuppence would feebly lick our hands as she regained consciousness, and try to wag her tail.

"The love of all living creatures," said Charles Darwin, "is the most noble attribute of man." Close contact with a pet is a first step toward that ideal. The pet is not an abstraction but an individual; its otherness, as well as its similarities, helps us to see ourselves as part of the animal kingdom. The short lifespans of these animals offer us a template for living a day at a time, humbly, taking nothing for granted, content with just enough, and for accepting death as part of life, to be faced quietly. Small wonder our pets wind themselves about our hearts so firmly that when they die there is a feeling of irreparable loss. Such love could not exist without respect, and in that lies the great hope; those we love and respect we do not harm, and once we feel that way about one animal, it is a short step to embracing them all.

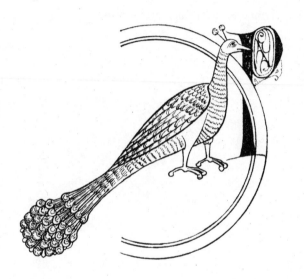

PEACOCKS AND LILIES, FOR INSTANCE

Something heavy thuds onto the roof. Then another something, and another, as if massive coconuts muffled in sacking are dropping on us from some virtual palm tree. This is followed by footsteps. From underneath, in my workroom, it sounds like a small platoon wearing particularly sturdy boots marching down the shingled slope. There is a pause, then one by one, from the eaves just above my window, the birds come into view as they launch themselves like hang-gliders and drift down, down to the neighbour's immaculate lawn below us on the hill. The peacocks are making their rounds.

When we moved to Victoria and were looking for somewhere to live, the peacocks sold us on the house we eventually bought. We had done the usual treks with the realtor, viewing houses in varying states of repair, slowly revising our price range upwards to accommodate the ones that had at least some of our requirements without needing extensive renovation. One house stood out—old, but commanding an impressive view of the ocean and Mount Baker—but someone had already made an offer on it. The prospective buyers kept adding further conditions, however, so the sale had not been finalized. If the buyers were to send a revised contract back to the seller yet again, the seller could refuse and we would have the opportunity to make an offer.

That was exactly how it turned out. One evening, Alan and I sat in our car on the quiet cul-de-sac while the realtor haggled on our behalf. A careless glance in my wing mirror made me gasp. Walking up the road were two peacocks, pacing side by side, heads turned as if they were deep in conversation. It was easy to think of them as two elder statesmen, dapper in morning suits and starched collars, deciding the fate of nations as they strolled, hands clasped behind their backs, in the formal gardens of some European palace—Lloyd George and Clemenceau perhaps, taking a break from hammering out the Treaty of Versailles.

Without a glance, the two birds passed the car and made their way toward the tangle of trees at the other end of the road. Their tails brushed the ground, swaying a little from side to side with each deliberate step; the blue of their necks was almost luminous in the dying light. It seemed immeasurably desirable to live in a place where peacocks wandered at will.

These beautiful birds have always been regarded as an adjunct to privilege, of course, a glamorous accessory to pride and power, valued precisely because they are extravagantly beautiful and serve no utilitarian purpose. They have decorated maharajahs' palaces; the Shah of Persia sat upon the Peacock Throne. They are predictable ornaments on the terraces of stately homes, filling the gardens and ravishing landscapes with their piercing cries. Carefully roasted, and reclothed in their plumage, they have graced the tables of emperors and kings, though if the twelfth-century bestiaries are to be trusted, they are a feast for the eye rather than the stomach. "His flesh is so hard," they say of the bird, "that it is scarcely subject to putrefaction, and it is not easily cooked." Perhaps, like thousand-year-old eggs and rotted narwhal, they are only for sophisticated palates.

In my own case, peacocks are bound inextricably with my childhood memories of wandering alone about Buscot Park, in Berkshire, on the enchanted Saturdays when my father was there on business.

We were predisposed, then, to embrace the resident peacocks when we moved into our new home, but I never imagined how absorbing they would turn out to be.

The first revelation was that our initial sighting of the two peacocks was the aberration, not the norm. We would have glimpses of the second bird, an immediately recognizable shape roaming across the fields below us, sometimes stalked by the neighbour's ginger cat at a respectful distance, but the bird who began to make daily visits was always alone, and, we thought, lonely.

His days seemed to consist of patrolling the neighbourhood in a constant search for food. We would see him in the gardens scratching under bushes, nipping at shoots, pecking at the ground, behaving exactly like a giant hen, and indeed, his legs and scaly feet with their large claws could have belonged to any supersized chicken. "Turkey!" was my small grandson's cry when he first saw the bird, and turkeys they have remained in our private parlance ever since.

We regaled the bird at first with what came to hand—bread, whole wheat to give it some claim to nutritional value—and made enquiries about the proper diet of peafowl. Nobody seemed to have much idea, not even the vet. The peacock enjoyed the bread anyway; he came regularly for handouts, so regularly that he quite overcame his initial skittishness and would take pieces from my hand.

We gave him a name, of course. Other neighbours had their own names for him—Charlie, and Fred, for instance—but we opted for alliteration and dignity, and called him Percy the Peripatetic Peacock.

In good weather Percy found a perch in the oak tree, or on the railing of the balcony outside my workroom. Both allowed ample dangling room for his tail. I could sit at my computer and watch him preening those miraculous feathers, burrowing under his wings, coiling the muscular electric-blue neck to riffle through the partly raised eyes on his back, realigning the barbs on the primary feathers by running them through his beak in a graceful sinuous flourish, and finishing with a brisk all-over shake, after which his tousled feathers quietly subsided into place, immaculate.

He did not always look that way. Winter took its toll. Mature peacocks shed all their long tail feathers in rapid succession in the fall, and though the new feathers step forward immediately to replace them, rather like sharks' teeth, it takes several months for them to reach their full length. For a time every year, peacocks walk around in a state of semi-nudity, truncated, or trailing one or two old tail feathers, usually broken or bent. It almost seems as if they feel embarrassed by the loss; generally they keep to themselves at this time and rarely put in an appearance.

When it rained, or when it was very cold and we had the few days' snow that is Victoria's usual ration, Percy was forlorn. We would come upon his bedraggled form crouched inside the carport, or under hedges, or hunched miserably on one leg beneath our neighbour's balcony, pretending to sleep. On days when the rain fell like rods from a steely sky, he would hardly venture out at all until late in the afternoon to search for food, announcing his presence with despairing hoots. At the sight of me breaking up a slice of bread, he would break into an ungainly run, honking urgently and snatching the pieces from my hands. He seemed cruelly remote from the heat of his native land (not that he'd ever seen it, of course), like a king driven into shabby exile, alone and yearning and forever dependent on the pity of others. I hoped he had somewhere dry and relatively warm to roost; I knew he could fly into the fir trees at the end of the road, but I'd never penetrated the mystery of where he went at night.

Spring brought its own transformations, pulsing along every vein, including Percy's. Darkness was shattered by his calls at three o'clock in the morning. The Roman writer Epiphanius would have us believe that this was because Percy was humiliated by his feet: "When he sees his feet," he says, "he screams wildly, thinking that they are not in keeping with the rest of his body." I can testify that at close quarters the wildness is startling and utterly fails to suggest self-loathing. Its effect was to remind us of the existence of the other peacock when he replied in kind, and the two of them launched into long-distance shrieking contests. Percy started practising his display at every opportunity. Often I would wake to the muted whirring of his tail feathers under my bedroom window, or see him on the lawn next door solemnly doing his edgewise dance—the quick turn, the shivering of the fan, the drooping of the wing feathers— for the benefit of indifferent rabbits.

The peacock's display is mesmerizing, no matter how familiar a sight it is, and not least because it is so unabashedly sexual. I was on my knees weeding in the front garden one day when I became aware of Percy stealing up behind me. His perfect fan was already unfurled, gently billowing in a slight breeze. The small head with its crown of tiny tufted blue feathers sat rigid atop the column of his neck, framed by the extravagant blues and greens of his body, an Elizabethan courtier with eyes like wet black stones. His gaze was intent, almost as if he were a mute compelling my attention by the sheer force of his will.

One step at a time, he edged closer, such a menacing, deliberate approach that a flutter of apprehension rippled in my stomach. When he was close enough for the edge of his fan to brush against me as it undulated, he stopped and inclined his head slightly. His beak parted. There was a faint noise, a silvery rustling, as he vibrated each tail feather along its entire length, a susurration that gained in intensity until it became visible sound, the shivering so rapid that the individual filaments of the feathers blurred. Then he turned his back on me, sweeping the fan around like a Victorian lady managing the train on her ball gown, and ruined the effect from my point of view (but not his own) by revealing his downy posterior.

It is a bravura performance, and the peacock's sole raison d'être. From the moment he hatches, every scrap of food he finds goes toward the gradual accumulation of magnificent feathers, from the very first specks of colour on neck and breast to the last notched finial on his longest tail feather, just so that he can sweep every female in sight off her scaly feet and father as many chicks as possible. That is literally all he does; he certainly has nothing whatever to do with raising the young, and once the eggs have hatched, the females want nothing more to do with him.

Percy's lovelorn performances were all the more pathetic, therefore, since he was entirely alone except for the other frustrated male whom he could only regard as a rival. His search for surrogates was sad, but it was also ludicrous, much as his powder-puff backside was the laughable reverse of his glorious display. If you're not the one experiencing its transports, maybe passion always has its ridiculous side. Certainly the spectacle of Percy sidling with intent up to rabbits was funny.

Years ago I read of a peacock in a zoo who caused great amusement by persistently displaying for a piece of topiary in the shape of a peacock. "Peacock Falls for Hedge" was the headline, and the piece played the situation for laughs, inviting us to smile at the idea of a creature dumb enough to be deceived by an artifact, tricked into courting a bush. It jarred me: how many of those chuckling patronizingly at the story were immune to deception in love? How many had made themselves ridiculous by their persistence in a lost cause?

In any case, the writer had got it all wrong. In order for humans to recognize it as a peacock, rather than simply a bird, the bush must have been clipped into the shape of a peacock with its fan erect—a male bird, in that case. The unfortunate subject of the report was reacting to the familiar silhouette of a rival on his turf, a particularly stubborn and baffling one, which made no sound, never ate, never once lowered its tail and refused to budge an inch. Far from being in love, I imagine that peacock was beside itself with frustration and rage, desperate to drive the monster away and failing, day after day. But there wouldn't have been anything to laugh at in that.

About two years after we moved in, a young man next door, clearing out the house after the death of his father, took pity on Percy. One afternoon, he and a friend appeared in the garden with a large box. Percy was sitting on the roof. They opened the box and urged the occupant to emerge. After a few seconds, a peahen stepped hesitantly onto the grass and looked around.

A frantic scrabbling from above announced that Percy had noticed. He thudded down the slope of the roof, teetered over the gutter, and leaped off, planing down into the garden, tail rippling, to land right beside the female and immediately start little circling rushes around her, head lowered. She ignored him and paced resolutely downhill. They disappeared through a gap in the hedge, Percy still weaving about her as if wrapping her in his charm, and descended into the field below. Another dark shape was emerging from the trees at the edge of the field, and soon the two males were pirouetting and fluttering, while the female, pecking at the ground in a desultory way, pretended they were both invisible in the ancient cruelty of her kind. That was the last we saw of any of them for several days.

Then another neighbour, possibly inspired by the first import and wishing to improve the odds for both males, introduced three more hens. Where we had once had just one lonely bird and fleeting glimpses of another, we now had two randy males and four females. The inevitable happened. We had no idea where they nested; all we knew was that one day, one of the females appeared with four brown chicks in tow, and then a second one introduced another little brood. The babies were all the same anonymous brown and very tiny compared to their giant mothers.

Very vulnerable, too.

We knew our area was a predator's heaven: a valley in the Agricultural Land Reserve full of riding stables and dairy farms, with wide, open fields for hay and grazing surrounded by hedges and groves of trees. The eagles and hawks circle endlessly, sometimes joined by turkey vultures, crows, ravens, and seagulls. Owls nest in nearby parks. On the ground, there are less visible but no less active dangers: raccoons, for instance, and rats, mink, weasels, and cats. The odds are not good for fledglings that spend most of their time on the ground, even though, as we discovered to our amazement, they were able to fly up into the branches of the massive fir tree across the road to roost.

The number of babies dwindled one by one, until there were just two left. Somehow they managed to evade disaster and quickly grew out of fluffy infancy. Looking back, it seems they were lucky to have hung on just long enough for the adult females to set aside all other duties and form their winter sisterhood. Once that happens, and the females move about in a gang, there is no shortage of extra watchful eyes and reasonably tolerant babysitters.

A pecking order prevails within the group, naturally. Age and length of residence bring respect, as does producing young that survive. There is a certain amount of deference when feeding time comes, a certain amount of bullying and chasing of the lowest on the totem pole, but as long as the internal rules are observed, the group spends the winter months in harmony, presenting a united front to the world.

The peahens are, in fact, a tribe of Amazons. The two males were ruthlessly excluded, and the more reclusive individual disappeared into the woods once more. Percy hung around, but endured bad-tempered nips and hostile attacks by several females at a time; they rushed at him with their own sturdy fans of tail feathers raised threateningly. Rejection kept him firmly marginalized, lurking abjectly just out of sight until the females had finished eating, then emerging to see if they had left him anything.

Since the females were dominant, at least for a time, it was possible to study them at close quarters. So often dismissed as dowdy, they revealed a beauty no less startling than the males', but one that whispers and invites the hand to its softness rather than trumpets glory and dazzles the eye. Instead of electric blue, their necks are a lovely sea green, the colour echoed in some of the tiny feathers of their coronets. Their breasts are cream, speckled with large darker spots, rather like a thrush, and the feathers on their backs are a soft brown, filigreed with cream and darker brown. The whole effect is lacelike, as delicate as the wavering patterns of lichen on stone, utterly different from the gorgeous colours and patterns of the male. The primary feathers are a rich chestnut and the tail is dark brown.

Daily visits soon enabled us to tell them apart. Each had individual characteristics, of appearance or behaviour. There was a matriarch, who led the charges against Percy and menaced the cats with a look, one step in their direction and a staccato "Took!" There was one with a limp, and another with a single white primary feather on her right side. There were the two babies, now gawky teenagers, both female, almost as large as their mother, but still following her around as she gently clucked and wheezed at them, indicating food on the ground with her beak and standing back as they pecked it up. And there was the Interloper, a female who just appeared one day and tagged along to the barely concealed irritation of the management. In a year, the tribe had grown from two lone birds to nine.

Inevitably, the courtship rituals the next year were even more frenzied. Calls filled the air at all hours; the oak tree, a favourite roost for the Amazons, would erupt in alarmed fluttering and stumbling around the branches in the middle of the night; at every turn, I came across Percy dancing for an audience or rehearsing on his own, valiantly maintaining his dignity in spite of heartless females with mundane priorities who sneaked behind him to browse on the ragged remnants of the cuticle-like sheath that protected his new tail feathers as they grew. The burden of greater numbers to impress may have tipped Percy into paranoia; whatever the reason, he now saw rivals everywhere, and mounted a campaign to eliminate them.

My car was one of his chief victims. Percy spent hours stalking round and round the vehicle, staring fiercely into the eyes of his reflection. When intimidation had no effect, he would leap at his rival, trying to rake him with formidable claws and spurs. The persistence of the dull thuds told me that Percy was single-minded about this and unlikely to give up. I had nowhere to store the car out of sight, so I had to come up with a way of eliminating the reflection that was driving him mad. A well-used off-road vehicle gave me an idea. I made a slurry of peat moss and water and daubed it onto the bottom part of the car. It looked awful, but effectively removed the gloss. Alan was embarrassed to ride in it, but Percy lost all interest in my car and turned his attention elsewhere.

The car belonging to a private nurse working at a house down the road was an inviting silver which made an excellent mirror. Soon she was battling an obsessed peacock. I could hardly suggest daubing mud all over her vehicle; this time we rigged a temporary dress for the car out of old sheets held together with clothespins. Again it looked dreadful, but it saved the car from damage, and more importantly, prevented the nurse from refusing to attend the house because of ravening wildlife.

This incident emphasized the complex nature of the peacocks' relationship with the residents on the road. Most of them liked the peacocks. Like me, they probably felt the birds added a touch of the exotic to our quiet, conventional neighbourhood. Like me, they probably enjoyed smiling as visiting drivers stood on their brakes and gawped at the sight of us knee deep in birds, feeding them by hand. Tradesmen, Fed Ex drivers, the men who read the meters and delivered the propane, Jehovah's Witnesses, all were diverted from their purpose when they saw Percy and the Amazons. "There are peacocks on your roof," they'd marvel, and we'd take a secret pleasure in being able to make the nonchalant reply, "Oh, they're always around; they just go where they like." More problematic was the frequent question, "What do they *do*?" but they'd nod, smiling, as if a longing had been satisfied, when I answered, "Nothing; they just *are*."

Not everyone embraced them quite as thoroughly as we did. Some residents liked to see them around, but would never offer them food. Some liked the birds but didn't like the mess they made when they perched for any length of time on fences or balconies; they made perching uncomfortable or impossible with wire netting and similar obstructions. Two of the more anally retentive gardeners, who couldn't bear a blade of grass out of place, would chase away any peacocks attempting dust baths in their borders, or sampling the smorgasbord of newly planted annuals. The spectacle of elderly men lumbering after the birds on steep slopes, making ineffectual swipes at them with corn brooms, was entertaining, but only because they never actually made contact. They had made their feelings known, and the birds moved on, a little flustered but unscathed, until the next time. Somehow, humans and birds had worked out a complicated scale of acceptance and tolerance that seemed to satisfy everyone.

Except one.

The first inkling that something was going on was dramatic. Percy disappeared. One day he was there, screaming his challenge to all comers, pursuing his harem, thudding over roofs and preening in the oak tree, and the next he was gone, vanished in mid-twirl as it were. It dawned on us then that we hadn't seen the other male for a while, either.

The neighbourhood was suddenly quiet, but the forces that generate and spread information in any community were hard at work. From the gardeners who came every week to mow some of the lawns, my neighbour heard a disquieting story, which she instantly relayed to everyone else. The man who lived in the end house, they said, had built a trap with a mirror in it in his yard to catch the peacocks.

We seethed over this for several days. Finally, Alan did the obvious thing. He marched to the end house, peered into the yard, saw the trap, and knocked on the door. Alan would not flourish in the diplomatic service and the confrontation was waspish on both sides. Yes, the man said, he had trapped the peacocks. Why? Because he didn't like them coming into his yard and he could do what he liked on his property. And what had he done with them? He had taken them to Nanaimo.

He had taken them to Nanaimo? In the welter of possible considerations, such as the legal positions in question, relevant bylaws, the potential involvement of the SPCA and the Capital Regional District, never mind the trauma inflicted on the birds by using their own instincts as a weapon against them, and the sheer bloody-minded self-centred unilateral unneighbourly to-hell-with-everybody-else effrontery of it all, I found myself mulling over this one statement. How? my mind kept asking. In the trap? But a trap big enough to contain a male peacock would be a formidable burden to pick up single-handed, and transferring an irate bird from a trap to another container would be dangerous. Even professionals like animal protection officers are very reluctant to handle peacocks because of their spurs and claws. And if he managed this somehow, what did he do then? Drive over sixty miles to tip Percy out at the side of the Island Highway, again without sustaining any injury, and drive away? Somehow I couldn't believe it. The alternative, which was sickening, I could.

We pursued the matter. The police said there was nothing they could do and sent us to the regional district's animal shelter. The officers were sympathetic and concerned, but shook their heads; while there are regulations about the treatment of wild and domestic animals or pets, creatures like the peacocks, which are semi-domesticated but belong to nobody, fall through the cracks. There was nothing they could do, either, unless the offender had moved the animals from his property. But the only way of proving that might have happened would be to search the landfill, or go to Nanaimo, somehow locate some peacocks, and find one that would take bread from our hands. We had to accept the fait accompli.

It was a souring experience. In a street with just eleven houses, it was impossible to ignore, but in the way of people who make a virtue of minding their own business and keeping themselves to themselves, the residents just muttered a lot and pointedly turned their backs in a typically futile way. The culprit was quite unmoved by disapproval; to be capable of such egocentricity, he would have to be impervious to everything except his own comfort, anyway. In a conflict that pits the ordinary person against anyone of sociopathic tendencies—one who heeds only the rules or conventions that benefit him—the outcome is inevitable, and even if there is some fallout, as in the case of the woman who poisoned the trees that spoiled her view of English Bay in Vancouver, the damage is done. Percy and his cohort were gone forever, disposed of like garbage, and we were all the poorer for it. Now, it seemed, the females were dwindling, too, in sympathy.

We had got used to having only one or two immature females about, when one day I saw a familiar limping form leading four tiny chicks. Soon after, another family appeared, and another. We were overjoyed to see them, but of course, the same relentless imperatives quickly reduced their numbers, and it seemed that most of the original females had disappeared. By late summer we were left with two mothers with two chicks each and a couple of yearling females. By early fall, one of the mothers had disappeared, and her orphan chicks straggled miserably in the wake of the others. Miraculously, they managed to survive as hangers-on in the little group, just large enough to fend for themselves, and benefiting from group security and the watchful sentries who hooted in alarm at the first sign of trouble.

They had the last laugh. I had learned that male chicks develop barred tail feathers when they've grown out of the uniform brown anonymity of infancy. To my delight, I realized that of the chicks, we had two females and two males. One of the females inherited the single white wing feather of her mother. Sadly, one of the males disappeared over the winter, and today there are only four peacocks altogether, but the remaining male, now eighteen months old, is slowly acquiring the eyes on his back and tail feathers. He is still accepted in the group, but he spent this summer shrieking and practising his dance, and by next year his female relatives will probably exile him to solitary bachelorhood.

The gene pool has shrunk, the numbers are precarious given all the natural hazards they encounter daily, and their chances of survival are limited at best, but they continue to come twice a day for their wheat seed and cracked corn. Visitors still marvel, compelled, whether they realize it or not, to arrest the swift current of their days in homage to a beauty whose only purpose is to adorn the world. I track the birds' wanderings about the gardens and fields, listen for their calls and the sound of their footsteps on the roof, pick up the feathers they shed as they sit in the oak tree, preening, and wait for the time when the soft shudder of a peacock's fan once again summons me from sleep on another morning in the spring of the year.

SWANS

Long ago, when I was a gawky schoolgirl, I played field hockey for my school. Naturally, team practices were a regular feature of that short period between the end of classes and the dying of the light over the autumn and winter months.

We were fortunate in our school grounds, which were large enough to provide a regulation-size hockey pitch and plenty of room to spare, bounded at the far end by a line of handsome old chestnut trees, and a little wild coppice, called The Spinney, which was deliberately left as nature intended. The whole expanse was a green oasis in a densely populated residential and light industrial area, close to major railway lines converging on nearby London.

During one of those hockey practices, I was running as usual down the left wing, shadowing the forwards with the ball, when I was distracted by a strange noise.

It kept time as unswervingly as a metronome. It was a rhythmical creaking, rather like an old-fashioned wood-and-leather bellows fanning the flames in a forge, a muffled sawing with the merest hint of a breathy whistle. At first I could not even make out where it was coming from, but as it got louder, I realized it was behind and above me. I stopped and looked up just in time to see a single swan flying about fifty feet over my head.

I had seen plenty of swans before. They crowded the River Thames near my home, posing like figurines on the water, and spoiling that image with their greed for handouts. But I had never seen one flying, never seen the long neck and head pointing the way, never realized that the flow of air passing over and through the feathers as the great wings flexed might be audible. Hearing that sound, strange to me and utterly familiar to the bird, made me feel for an instant as if I shared its mastery of the air, and I stood in a shock of delight, quite alone, while the rest of the players pounded to the other end of the field.

Swans made another arresting appearance in my life, much later and thousands of miles away, when I lived in northern British Columbia. Fort St. James is typical of rural settlements in the province: small, remote, lacking amenities and tied to a resource-based economy, now seriously depressed due to the pine beetle and the downturns in the forest industry. In compensation, like so many similar communities, the village has stunning surroundings. High on a plateau, it crouches at the southern tip of Stuart Lake with a long vista of blue and purple hills, of endless trees and small islands, stretching as far as the distant horizon.

Winter closes like a giant fist about the town, squeezing it relentlessly into numbness. The spruce trees crowd in; the sky gains weight and leans down, leaden. The water in the lake grows dark and still. Below skeletal branches the ground becomes iron as its heartbeat slows. The whole world holds its breath, waiting for the snow to fall and the ice to form.

On just such a day, the trumpeter swans would drop from the sky, pausing briefly in their migration south from their Arctic breeding grounds. I never saw them arrive; that was part of their magic. Overnight, it seemed, the sombre lake bloomed. The swans floated at rest, the graceful curves of neck and partly unfurled wing turning them into exquisite water lilies, rare and reassuring as all winter-flowering species are.

Before long, they would grow restless and resume their journey. The moment would come, at some imperceptible signal, and the necks would stretch out, the wings would beat, unhurried, hoisting the bodies so that the black feet could stride across the surface of the lake, faster and faster, until the lift snatched them free and the birds eased upwards as one, my heart leaping to join them. They would circle, gleaming against the infinite greys of water, rock, and sky, manoeuvring into long, V-shaped skeins, and their strange cries would ring and echo between the hills, a wild conversation that lingered on the air long after they were lost to the eye.

Their ultimate destination was quite likely to be Vancouver Island, where I now live, having followed their example and sought out a place where winter is an altogether kinder season. One of the first things I saw when I moved into the house and gazed at the view was a field below, full of white shapes. All that winter the swans flew past my windows every day on their way to and from the farms. I would make special journeys in the car to reach the fields where they spent their days, and stand at the fences watching them feeding on the grass and winter rye, or preening and resting while the sentries stood at the edge of the flock, heads high, watching every direction.

They are so big, so strong, so proud in flight, they seem invincible—even though lead poisoning from the shot buried in the sediment of the ponds and lakes where they feed threatens their existence. Their beauty is a perfection of form and simple grace, like that of a pearl. Appearing in the winter as they do, bringing their vividness to the drab days when the very impulse to life falters, they are portents of hope. The world may be dark, bedevilled with conflict and suffering, yet it has creatures like this to adorn it, quietly weathering the lean times in the certainty that there will be another spring, another journey, another hatching under a sun that never sets. My heart still skips, exultant, whenever I see them, just as it did on that hockey field so long ago, when the sound of wings turned my face skyward.

ANIMAL BEHAVIOUR

A Kleenex advertisement featuring a bespectacled man in saffron robes tenderly setting a little tortoise back on its feet and restoring a gasping goldfish to its pond resonates with me. The implied reverence for all living things makes my kind of sense.

I have always loved animals. That is easy to say, of course, but I would have thought my own claim was sturdier than mere sentimentality. More principled, even. I abhor hunting. Living close to Stuart Lake, just outside Fort St. James in northern British Columbia, we deliberately left acres of our own property untouched, to provide undisturbed habitat for wild animals and birds. Live and let live, I would have said, was inscribed indelibly on my heart.

But that was before the beavers.

When the spring runoff flooded the wood as usual that year, I was enchanted to see a beaver sculling about among the trees. By the end of the summer, though, I suddenly realized that the water level was still inordinately high, so high indeed, that the sump pump in the basement was growling at regular intervals. When one of our poplar trees fell onto the power lines at 7:29 one Sunday morning and hung, smoking, above the road while breakfasts came to an abrupt halt in the entire neighbourhood, the neatly chiselled stump of the casualty left no doubt of the culprit. Another tree close by was also freshly chewed and from the thicket behind the barn came the persistent sound of running water.

This called for investigation.

Penetrating the dense undergrowth, I found a disaster. Dark brown water like stewed tea lay everywhere, punctuated by ferns and a tangle of matted willow, nettles, and dogwood. Footing was treacherous: the ground was uneven and littered with fallen trees and branches, stumps and slippery leaves, all invisible; each step was threatened. Water was pouring down to the lowest point in several places. Huge poplars lay splayed in every direction; others, filed to a point, waited for a strong wind to push them over, while several had ominous piles of wood chips beside the fresh white wounds at their base.

I squelched through sodden grass, leaving deep footprints which filled rapidly, and clambered over logs, using them as bridges to higher, drier spots, aiming at the edge, the boundaries of this mess. The changed contours brought me finally to the bank of the creek, to a spot where the water was forcing a new channel through the bush to rejoin the stream, and I saw the dam and understood.

My heart sank. The beavers had tried before, farther downstream where the water was very shallow and the banks no height at all. It had been easy to discourage that attempt. But this! This was a complete obstruction, nearly four feet high, the work obviously of months. Another obstruction, a complete tree trunk, lay across the stream farther up. Between the two stretched a smooth expanse of water, unbroken except for tufts of grass and willow that marked what had once been the banks. The old margins had disappeared completely, and glints striking through the trees showed clearly enough the source of the alien waters rushing through the woods in search of depth.

I scanned the future. I could see the trees standing in ice and water all winter, slowly dying, asphyxiated, until all that remained were leafless skeletons, stark as the remains of a forest fire. I saw the shrews and mice forced out of their tunnels, and the snowshoe hares loping to higher ground. I saw the birds abandoning the branches that had given them shelter in winter and cover for their nests in spring, and heard the silence descending. A dreadful metamorphosis would transform our wood and creek into swamp: the only visitors lugubrious, solitary moose, the only sounds the slapping, booming, croaking, and quacking of a stagnant watery world.

And we had been thinking of putting the property on the market, too.

I felt like Rachel Carson visualizing the Apocalypse. Any action seemed better than inaction, no matter how futile. Armed with a three-pronged rake straight out of paintings of the Last Judgment, I made for the dam.

It was easy to approach. Barely covering the soles of my gumboots, the lackadaisical water trickled over round, slippery stones. The rampart of the dam sloped ahead of me, a bristling heap like a giant game of Pick-Up-Sticks.

Where to start?

The water, held in a curving meniscus at the lip of the dam, trickled over at several carefully controlled spots. These natural spillways seemed a good place to begin. I chose one in the centre and climbed the dam. I was surprised at how solid it felt, even though individual branches writhed or sagged underfoot, and pressure sometimes made them give way. One foot would be trapped between grasping forks and notches, causing panicky struggles as I tried to release myself without losing my boot. It was strange to stand on top of the dam and move along it, almost like walking on water, for the deep pool stretched far away from my feet, still and dark, a wall of silt sloping wanly down into the murk.

The longest journey begins with a single step. I selected a branch that poked from the tangle, almost offering itself. I pulled; it resisted. I pulled harder; it gave a little, but I knew that if I pulled again, it would yield suddenly and topple me from my perch. I shifted my foothold and approached it again, trying this time to dislodge other branches locking the first into place in a wooden embrace. They parted reluctantly, arthritic projections snagging and hooking, but finally free. I stood, gathering myself to fling the dripping, unwieldy lump as far onto the bank as possible. It was the first of many. I became a contestant in some demented Highland Games, tossing cabers like corkscrews with my feet nailed firmly to the ground. The futility of some of my throws, defeated by weight or catching on a nearby tree and tumbling straight back into the creek, made me giggle, but it was curiously satisfying, nonetheless, to destroy.

And there were results. As more branches came out, more water spilled over the rim. By the time I was standing in several inches that were hurrying in a determined way through the gap, the current was strong enough to roll large stones. There was excitement in the mass of water pressing forward to escape. I put my rake to work, dredging the silt, pushing out stones, tearing up the roots and thin twigs binding the dam together, scooping off great mats of dead leaves as they collected on the surface. The water gathered its forces and heaved at the rim, pushing aside smaller branches, cascading down, roaring in a torrent over, between, among, the dead weight tumbling to the floor of the creek, waking it up, scouring a new hole as it was impelled ever more fiercely along the bed.

Above the roar of the water I could hear the occasional loud slap on the surface. I looked, but ripples were the only evidence the beavers were about. The knowledge that they were watching gave an added savour to the work. By the time the sun went down I had a hole in the dam five feet across, and I waded back downstream with the water now tugging at my legs, close to slopping over the top of my boots.

But I had triggered formidable forces. By the next morning the creek had dwindled once more. Another gumbooted trek revealed the dam restored exactly as it had been the day before. It should have been an object lesson in futility but I was not going to capitulate to beavers. They may have had the pressing matter of winter food supply behind their activity, not to mention instinct, but I had my nightmare of the desolate swamp and a certain obstinacy goading me. Half of my brain told me I was stupid, wasting my time, banging my head against a brick wall. My persistence only gave my colleagues at the high school the opportunity to laugh at me and predict certain defeat. I knew they were right and went to war anyway.

The second day I saw the beavers for the first time. Both heralded their presence with loud slaps and made no attempt to watch me secretly.

All the time I was there, they patrolled the far end of their pool, swimming slow widths in opposite directions, their blunt snouts crisscrossing regularly. The third day, as I clambered on top of the dam, one beaver was swimming toward me, towing a large branch. For a few seconds we looked one another in the eye before I clapped my hands and startled it into dropping its burden and diving with a great sinuous heave, banging its rubbery tail like a carpet beater in protest. The fourth day, the beavers circled the pool, coming closer and closer to the dam, their irritation palpable. I felt a kind of glee at getting under their skin. By the fifth day of unrelenting deconstruction and reconstruction, they were provoked into direct intimidation.

I was widening a gushing hole in the top of the dam, deafened by the water and standing with my back to the pool, when I was thrown off balance by a mighty smack behind me. A beaver had silently paddled to within two feet before springing his surprise. My boots filled with water, my heart beat a little faster, and I thought suddenly of the unfortunate man who had been attacked by a seemingly befuddled beaver he had stopped to help on a bridge in a pelting rainstorm. I thought how amazingly big the first beaver I ever saw out of the water looked as it trundled slowly across the road, and imagined those great orange incisors locked like cold chisels in a meaty part of my leg. That round definitely went to the rodents.

But the campaign could not be abandoned. Indeed, it had acquired a momentum all its own. My concerns, laughable as they were, had roused others; Fish and Wildlife were alerted, somebody's brother-in-law who was a trapper expressed interest, there was talk of mounting a dam-busting party with bonfire and hot dogs. The conservation officer, overtaxed with bears roaming hungrily near homes, delegated a trapper to clear the creek. On the very afternoon I left the beavers with three huge torrents to stem, the troops were mobilized and the advance guard put in an appearance.

Suddenly I was no longer the lone warrior, locked in single combat, but more like the exhausted conscript, inadequately equipped, sent to the rear once the heavy artillery arrives.

The first casualties, victims of their own obsession, fell minutes after I had left the dam for the last time. I have no details of their end, but I imagine them, paddling energetically toward the holes, laden with building material, shot one by one as they approach. Three went that day, at least two more later in the week. After that, I did not enquire.

The water level in the wood dropped; no new trees were sharpened like huge pencils; the sump pump fell silent. Dry leaves fell into the creek and were swept away on the brisk current; the stream poured unresisted over the ruined dam. The campaign I started in the warm evenings of September had been won, but the triumph was flawed. Is this how generals feel as they survey the price of their victories lying on the battlefield?

The beavers had gone, but the solution could only be temporary. More enduring was the change in me. Before this I claimed to be an animal lover without blushing; even if I did not actively love some creatures, like spiders, I would at least give them a wide berth and leave them to get on with their lives, marvelling academically at their mysteries. But I could no longer pride myself on an acceptance of all living creatures; in the face of an inconvenience and a threat to the value of my property I manifested exactly the draconian reaction I deplore in others. Get rid of them, I said; I don't care how.

On their own, they would have defeated me hands down. I could only feel I cheated to call in help from people who were not burdened by sentiment, who could be ruthless for me. Against creatures that were merely being themselves I ranged all the resources of humans doing likewise. There was no satisfaction to be had in their disappearance, just a dispiriting sense of meanness. Even the concern for the wood and its creatures that first spurred me on felt tainted, suspect, contaminated by special pleading. In my own view I dwindled.

So in my mind the beavers linger, still swimming cleanly round their pool, carving bow waves with their heads. The rubber tails flail the silent water and they gaze, benignly stupid, down their aristocratic Roman noses. They make me very sad, but sadder yet is the knowledge that, another time, in similar circumstances, I would probably do exactly the same.

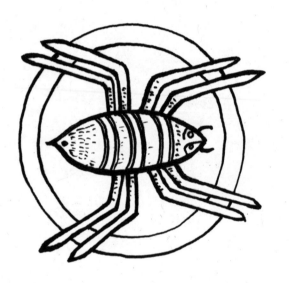

PHOBIA

She sits on my outstretched hand, filling the palm. Against my pale skin, she is matte black, except for the gleam of her strange, fierce eyes. Her eight legs are bunched up, motionless but ready, hinting at a speed belied by the plump body, covered with silky hairs, that looks as if it would yield like a down cushion to the slightest pressure.

To the eye she is substantial, almost meaty, yet I have already blurted out my surprise, like every other visitor who elects to hold her—"She's *so light!*" And she is: weightless, airy, the merest breath, a whisper of a presence on my hand.

Both of us are quite still: she, because she is apparently unafraid and disinclined to move; I, because I am afraid of startling her and dare not move. Only adults can hold her, they said; if she's dropped, she will explode. But how will I react if she runs?

I can hardly believe I am doing this.

I was always able to empathize with Miss Muffet. There is a very early memory involving a spider. At least part of my recollection springs from my mother's account, as I suspect many of our childhood memories do. Certainly I remember her telling the story with some relish, rather unkindly in my estimation, but the setting is perfectly clear in my mind's eye, sufficiently detailed to suggest that the experience was real and mine, as indelible in its own way as a name written with the purple-leaded pencils once used to mark the sheets sent off to the laundry.

We were visiting my grandmother. At the time she lived in Wisbech, an old market town in Cambridgeshire, close to the Norfolk border, set in the midst of low-lying black fields reclaimed from the sea hundreds of years before. The land is drained by slow-moving rivers and deep canals called cuts that slash through acres of sugar beet straight for the horizon. Solitary clumps of trees, huddles of yellow-brick houses and the bulk of extraordinarily large, lonely churches are the only things to stand in the way of the east wind off the North Sea. The place itself is not important, though it occupied a special place in my heart, being the very antithesis of my home in the suburbs southwest of London, but the fact that it was rural is. My grandmother had been born in a tiny Norfolk village a few miles away, had lived her entire life on farms, and had probably never moved much more than fifty miles in any direction from that starting point. She was a countrywoman, through and through.

As such, I suspect she harboured the traditional rural distrust and faint scorn for city dwellers, misguided foreigners all, clueless when it came to proper (read, country) ways. Certainly my mother thought she did, and since Mum a city girl from Kent, I guess she must have experienced this attitude personally. I cannot tell if my mother's conviction that Grandma felt she wasn't quite the thing was justified, but I know she felt like an outsider around the old lady. At least I was a fairly presentable grandchild. Most of the time.

At the time of this story, my grandfather had died and Grandma had moved into town, nearer her two daughters, to share a house with another elderly lady. It was one of a terraced row with a wooden-handled pump that spewed water into a stone sink in the scullery and a huge, black-leaded range that glowered like a prehistoric Aga stove in the kitchen. In the garden space at the back, adorned mainly by clumps of catnip, there was a scrupulously whitewashed outhouse and in the corner by the fence, a dilapidated trellis construction called the summer house.

There was nothing for me to do when we visited. We actually stayed with my aunt while we were in Wisbech, but daily calls on my grand-mother were obligatory. Grandma was a Primitive Methodist; trivial pursuits did not exist in her world, but I was allowed to wander into the garden, such as it was, to escape the desultory adult conversation and the stultifying primness of my grandmother's room. In this tiny gravelled desert I fashioned such entertainment as I could devise for myself.

So there I was in the summer house. It was off-puttingly dark and dusty, but it had a small bench inside, no doubt for the benefit of those who chose to contemplate the beauty of the catnip in the heat of the day. I sat in the musty twilight, playing one of the solitary games I was so good at—populating the shadows with the pupils of an entirely imagi-nary classroom, for example, doing all the voices, or conducting lengthy conversations between doctors and patients, or riding muscular, con-trary horses on vast plains, mastering them by sheer strength and gentle whispers in their ears. So absorbed was I that when something gently alighted on my head, I brushed at it absently, only to find when I lowered my arm that there was now a spider attached to my hand.

In my eyes it was huge. It was a sci-fi monster, a scout sent ahead by an invasion of alien mutants. In my own defence, I must add that the spiders commonly found in and around houses in Britain *are* large, with fat black bodies, spiky black legs and attitude.

I tried to shake it off, but it would not fall. Quite the reverse in fact.

It was setting out over my wrist. I shook my arm even more furiously, moaning now, and managed to dislodge it, but it dangled for a second, then reeled itself back on its invisible silk, and scuttled higher. It was the speed of those eight legs, the suddenness and unpredictability, that unhinged me, that and the fact that it had disappeared round the back of my upper arm and I could not see it anymore but I knew it was heading for my neck and my face and it was bound to burrow under my collar or in my hair and I wouldn't be able to reach it at all and who knew what it would do to me but it was going to be horrible because it was the most horrible thing I'd ever encountered and get it off me, get it off me, GET IT OFF!

By this time, according to my mother's account, because I was no longer in any state to recall details, I was screaming, deaf to every plea and reassurance. Did my grandmother, shaking her head in disapproval at all the fuss, locate the spider and dispatch it? My mother would have been queasy about doing this, but perhaps she found the courage. But she could not stop me shrieking in this shameful, abandoned way—not with reason, not with shouts of her own, nor smacks, nor warning shakes. Her last resort was cold water in the face, one shock to drive out another. Did she actually hold me over the stone sink and start pumping? Did the water wait, then spurt in little jets, then leap in a solid green ribbon from the spout onto my upturned face? I can feel it, sense the shock of the cold blow, the gasp, the abrupt silence, the struggle to avoid drowning as the water filled my nose and mouth, and the coughing and spluttering and self-pitying wailing that followed. Or did the threat alone end my hysteria?

Not my fear, though. That is entrenched, somewhere deep in the hard-wiring of my brain. There have been many occasions when that heart-arresting scuttle—always, for some reason, *toward* rather than *away*—has immobilized me. Or the familiar shape crouched on the bottom of the bath has rendered showers impossible until some hardier soul has dealt with the intruder. I plead guilty to killing and injuring numerous spiders in my youth, lashing out in a desperate attempt to rid my space of aliens, knowing that my fear is irrational, but unable to conquer it.

I still blush to remember the night I found a large spider in my bedroom, when I was fifteen or so. I tried to deal with it myself with the weapons at hand, notably an encyclopedia, walloping the spider as it galloped across the floor, but its response was to curl up in a ball of legs as it was banged into the carpet, then quickly unfold when I cautiously lifted the book to see how successful I had been, to continue its march toward me. I was soon pressed against the wall opposite the door, convinced that I had met The Spider Who Could Never Die. My father had to get up and rescue me. I never lived it down.

But I would never have been able to sleep in that room, either, knowing that the spider was there. Irrational though such fear is—and even then my brain told me that those spiders were harmless, even benign, and I really had nothing to fear from them—it is still a genuine terror. It is not in the same league as those fears learned from experience; any sensible person stung by wasps or bitten by a dog would be cautious about wasps and dogs for life. Fear of spiders (or mice or snakes or frogs or even small birds and moths) is an instinctive response, a deep prompting of the amygdala buried in the most primitive part of the brain, an inheritance from our reptilian past. This is where true panic lies, paralysis of intellect and abject surrender to sensation, the reflex of the animal protecting itself.

I am convinced that it is mainly a visceral response to a particular kind of movement. The animals responsible for our most irrational fears are all capable of sudden bursts of great speed for their size: watch a spider rise from a crouch, rather like a classic Citroen, and scurry across a carpet on the very tips of its legs; the peculiarly oily slither of a snake seeking cover, or slaloming across a pond; the panicky scamper of mice and the random fluttering of birds and moths. Then there is appearance. Insects, arachnids, reptiles, amphibians, and birds are so patently unlike humans, so foreign with their odd anatomies, extraordinary coverings, whiplash tongues, multi-faceted eyes, external skeletons, hollow bones and bizarre eating habits—so difficult for Disney to render cute and cuddly. When the movement is attached to such a creature, what we experience is a confrontation with a threatening life form which might do anything at all, because there is no way to read it as one would a fellow human. Our response is as unthinking and understandable as my dog's, barking herself into a frenzy at a leather belt coiled on a chair, and just as hard to modify.

But it can be done.

Years later, back at my aunt's house once more, I stood rooted in front of her winter jasmine. Safely attached to the vine and the trellis it grew on, a spider was building a web in front of my fascinated eyes. She had already managed to stick the first thread to two points and was running back and forth, reinforcing it with additional silk. Then she unspooled a longer thread that she allowed to hang from the first like a limp clothesline. Quickly she added more, like a frame, and returned to the middle of the clothesline to drop, trailing silk, to the bottom of the frame, transforming the clothesline into a Y. Now she added radiating threads from the branch of the Y, travelling down each new one to unreel the next, her busy feet attaching it farther along the frame, then running back up it to start again at the middle with the next radius. That done, she started the circular threads near the centre, pausing at each radiating thread to sew a connection, spiralling farther and farther out until the framework was full.

I watched her until she was satisfied with her work and settled in the centre of the completed web, front feet delicately poised on the threads. I had no idea how long it had taken—an hour, maybe—but I could not have moved. I felt as if the spider had set a tiny door ajar, allowing me, Alice-in-Wonderland-like, one eye pressed to the opening, to spy on her reality, the mundane fashioning of a necessary tool for her, a miracle of design and ingenuity for me. It marked a change in my attitude to spiders; I will not go out of my way to find them, and I know that they still have the power to make me afraid if they get too close when I have no avenue of escape, but I marvel at their skill. I hug the memory of watching the web grow before my eyes to myself, knowing, perhaps, that others might not find the same wonder in it, and that the telling might tarnish that hour even for me.

There have been other insights in this long process of developing tolerance. I can remember my delight when the patch of tiny yellow and black beads massed together on the Montana Rubens clematis that covered the garage broke apart as fluidly as spilled mercury and revealed itself to be a huddle of baby spiders, hundreds of them, just hatched from the silken cocoon their mother had made to cover her eggs. Just as quickly they coalesced again, a myriad of pin head-sized organisms, all perfectly recognizable as miniature arachnids, all just as competent as their parents at unspooling silk and launching themselves onto the breeze, as trusting as parachutists on their first jump.

Then there was the nature program I saw on television. It was not one of the kind that pretends to be scientific but secretly exploits the unloveliest characteristics of its subject, the result being more like a B horror movie—*Attack of the Killer Wolf Spiders*, perhaps, with the same ten-second footage of the arachnid leaping out of its hole at a hapless victim repeated endlessly to creepy music and breathless narration. Rather it was one distinguished by its willingness to let the animals speak for themselves and by the brilliance of its photography. It was about spiders of every kind, all around the world, in every imaginable habitat: spiders that dug sand traps, fashioned webs like funnels or clouds of spun sugar, survived in deserts or in the pitch dark, ate their mates or lived for months without food, stunned their prey or killed a man with a single bite. The one that held me spellbound was a water spider, operating beneath the surface of a pond but still needing oxygen to breathe, clasping the gleaming pearl of an air bubble like a gypsy bent over her crystal ball. The image that abides is of the same spider, holding her web with two front legs, and casting it just like a fisherman throwing his net, floating it out into a perfect circle and drawing it back, over and over, balletic, hypnotic, unnervingly perfect.

With knowledge, then, fear may dwindle. There is not enough knowledge in the world, however, to transform this kind of apprehension into love, or even liking. While there are some people who can apparently feel the same affection for a tarantula as I would for a dog or cat, and actually keep them in their houses as pets, which seems as perverse in its own way as raising an alligator in the bathtub, there must be many more, like me, who can never hurdle the divide between respect and togetherness.

Forcing intellect into action, we arrive at a sort of tolerance, possibly even admiration, but it is at arm's length. We may tell ourselves firmly that the spider is our ally in ridding the house of flies and mites, and leave the web in place, complete with its cargo of carefully mummified victims. We may resist the conviction that the spider crawled up the drainpipe to terrorize us and believe that it went down for a drink only to be trapped at the bottom of sheer porcelain cliffs, and rescue it in an ample duster rather than turning on the tap and drowning it. We may watch over the egg cases as carefully as the mother spider herself, and cheer when the spiderlings first bungee-jump into the world. But don't let a spider drop suddenly onto our shoulders from a branch, or run over our foot, or dangle in front of us when we are grovelling under the sink or in the shadowy crawl space beneath the house. Rationality will not stand the strain.

Wherever spiders have made their mark in world culture, you will find the same ambivalence, as if humans have never quite been able to make up their minds about these strange creatures. Arachne, certainly a star of the arachnid universe, can be seen in two ways: either the master weaver of the Greek myth, whose work even Envy declared "without flaw," the victim of a sore loser who happened to be a goddess; or the vainglorious braggart whose claim to be superior to Athena, while it was no less than the truth, exhibited a hubris that simply asked to be squelched. Anansi, the mythological West African spider, is a benefactor to humans but often, like Raven, a mischievous, self-serving trickster. For every Charlotte, using her web in Wilbur's defence and quietly educating him about the mysteries of life and death, there is an Aragog terrifying Harry Potter. For every Spider Woman, creating the world by thought and showing the Navajo the Way of Beauty, there are the armies of arachnids, including shiny silver robots with clacking pincers, swarming across movie screens intent on bringing civilization as Hollywood knows it to an end.

Carting this baggage, I follow the docent around the exhibits in the Bug Zoo. With my four-year-old granddaughter, I am whiling away a rainy afternoon in Victoria in the company of creatures that I would normally avoid, as would most of the other visitors, particularly the adults, judging by their expressions and the way they hang behind their children. We have investigated the huge ant colony, allowed the giant millipede (which tickles like the bristles of a nylon scrub brush) to ripple across our hands, stroked the hissing cockroaches, tried to outstare the passionless gaze of the leaf-green praying mantis, and counted the stick insects hanging on their twigs. Now we are standing in front of a small glass tank containing some sand, a few rocks and a tarantula, and I am faced with a dilemma.

"She's very gentle and quiet," says the docent, an enthusiastic biology student from the local university, "but I can only let the grown-ups hold her because she's very fragile. If you drop her, she'd explode on impact. Who'd like to be first?"

It is a challenge. The adults turn shifty-eyed, and break out in weak smiles. Some take a step back. The children stare at us. What to do? Should I join this lily-livered bunch and stay silent? Isn't this the perfect opportunity to press the limits of my hard-won tolerance of spiders? Wouldn't I prove something to myself as well as to the four-year-old at my side?

A hand stretches out and I hear, "I'll hold her." Unaccountably, it is my voice and my hand.

I don't know what I was expecting. Not this weightless creature, slightly warm, trustingly filling my palm. I want to touch the hair, I would like to feel a leg (a foot?) stir on my skin, I wish I could look closely at the multiple eyes while I have the chance, but the thought of that soft body breaking apart, the mess of fur and broken legs and whatever spiders have inside them, turns me to stone. The children lean in to peer at her, their parents take photographs of my hand, and the steadiness of that hand astonishes me. Still, it is a relief when the docent takes the spider back and tenderly sets her down in front of her rocks. When the others turn away to the scorpions, I linger by the tarantula for a moment. I feel absurdly proud of myself, as if I've measured up to something in my own mind. What it is, however, I'm not sure; the spider still looks to me like the stuff of nightmare even though she is immobile, and I'm glad she is confined to a glass box. The hysterical child has come a long, long way, but she is not ready to fold spiders to her heart, not yet.

And what of my granddaughter? Did screwing my courage to the sticking point have the desired effect on her? Impossible to tell, at the time. She was inscrutable, in the way of four-year-olds one would like to impress. But just the other day she rushed into my kitchen to tell her mother about the spider she'd seen running about the web it had constructed over the bin where I keep grain for the peacocks.

"Be careful," she commanded as we all dutifully admired the little golden-brown spider. "You mustn't break its web. It's just waiting for its dinner."

I think she has the right idea.

BATS

I am not good at heights, but my husband gets sweaty palms watching the Ferris wheel scene in *The Third Man*, so there I was, at the very top of our fully extended extension ladder, about to paint the highest wall of our house. The ground sloped in more than one direction and I was relying on a perilous arrangement of wood chocks and flat stones to keep the ladder upright. To reach the pointed bit at the gable end I had climbed several rungs beyond the place where I could comfortably hold onto the ladder for support, and my legs were trembling with the strain. Knees locked, head inches away from a louvred vent, one hand inching the paintbrush toward the paint can hanging from the other, I was talking to myself in a breathy little voice, "OK, come on, you can do it, just this little bit, then you can go lower down, take it slowly, no hurry . . ." Then something moved in front of my nose.

Between two of the louvres there was a face. It was straight out of Goya's nightmares, grotesque and fuzzy, because I was too close to it to focus clearly, but as I jerked back instinctively (and dangerously) I saw that Hieronymus Bosch could well have designed it, a savage little demon face at home in hell, spiteful, needle teeth bared. A brown leathery wing groped into view, a tiny claw at one bony joint dragging it forward, and suddenly the creature slipped past my head without a sound.

That was my first evidence that we had resident bats.

There were plenty around. One of the drawbacks of rural living in northern British Columbia during the summer is the abundance of insect life; at times the mosquitoes would drive us indoors or compel us to put up mesh-walled tents in order to enjoy warm summer evenings in the open air. Far worse were the blackflies. No refined hypodermic to syphon our blood for them; equipped with mandibles to bite out small chunks of flesh, they furtively crawled round the hairline, into ears, or behind knees, leaving trails of blood as their calling cards. Mowing a lawn became an assault course through a hailstorm of blackflies, rousted from their cozy sanctuaries in the grass, all with an appetite for revenge and the ability to make their victims feverish and cranky with their bites.

Misery for us, but paradise for insectivores. Every summer, toads flourished; swallows and martins patrolled tirelessly; and when each long day faded and the birds flew to roost, bats materialized in the twilight like a ghostly changing of the guard.

We cheered them on. When mosquitoes and blackflies make life miserable, it is hard not to feel affection for a creature that consumes three times its body weight in insects every day. Wonder, too, at the miraculous guidance system that allows it to operate in the dark with the accuracy of a heat-seeking missile. Their hunting prowess alone qualifies them as remarkable animals; when you add in their amicable communal living arrangements, their devotion as parents and their babysitting provisions for their young, they seem altogether admirable.

Our admiration would have remained academic—just the result of having our interest piqued by their presence, and informed by the simplest of research—if I hadn't discovered, one sleepy afternoon, that the lone animal I had encountered earlier was not an aberrant hermit; we had bats, so to speak, actually living in our belfry. I was lounging on the deck, almost reading a book, floating on a quiet like a held breath, when I became aware of a noise. A very small noise, a tiny chittering, somewhere above my head. There weren't too many options for the source: a blank wall, broken only by a French window that led into my kitchen, and above that, yes, another one of those louvred openings backed by wire mesh that ventilated the attic.

At first I couldn't see anything. Then I realized that the outer side of the wire mesh behind the louvres was moving and squeaking. I had discovered the bats' dormitory. They were hanging from the mesh in a space I would have thought far too narrow for comfort and much too hot, since it faced south, but apparently it suited them, for there they stayed every summer.

I could never count them. Their fur was exactly the same colour as the mesh, and while the ones that turned over in bed were easy to spot, there were plenty more who never budged, no matter how noisy their brethren were or how many elbows jabbed into their ribs. The only time I could estimate their numbers was at twilight, and even then my eyes were not always sharp enough to catch them as they flew out.

I took to watching their evening launch. After sunset, I would sit at the edge of the deck, parallel to the wall of the house so that I could see the bats against the clear sky as they emerged, and wait. They would stir as the light faded; I would hear them talking, scratching about on the mesh, growing more and more restive as the sky darkened. At some unfathomable moment, some conjunction of light and heat and will discernible only to the bats, they would leave their sleeping quarters one by one in rapid succession, each distinctive silhouette slipping down and away as if they were being poured into the night.

Sometimes, open doors would seduce them into the house and we would watch, bemused, as they executed figures of eight about the rooms, weaving round the furniture, following the walls and ceilings and floors without so much as grazing them, changing direction in a heartbeat and without any slackening of pace. We would turn off the lights and open the windows and doors; in no time they would find the way out and leave as silently as they had entered. Left alone, the bats were infallible.

Which is why I was appalled to hear a colleague at school talking about her adventure with a bat.

Louisa was standing in the empty staff room long after the last bell, talking to another teacher. I hadn't heard the very beginning of the conversation but I was soon eavesdropping shamelessly. Louisa was already excited by her own narrative; her voice, always penetrating and relentlessly jolly, was rising to the drama.

"...and the kids were so scared, flapping about it was, and you couldn't tell where it was going next, Mum shouting, 'Get it out, get it out!' I didn't know what to do, I didn't really want to get anywhere near it, what if it got tangled up in my hair? Anything could have happened, and the kids were screaming, so I shut them in the bathroom with Mum, and I got a broom and a bucket and I went after it. Well, I chased it all over the house, but I gave it a good whack finally, knocked it onto the floor in the kitchen, and before it could get away again I put the bucket over it."

Her eyes were shining. "Then I called my brother next morning and he came over and killed it with a shovel."

She regarded her audience expectantly, obviously anticipating approval, congratulation, admiration—acknowledgment of her narrow escape, at least. I was imagining the bat's terror, its disorientation in the midst of the humans' hysterical racket, its frantic attempts to evade the flailing broom, its imprisonment, probably injured, in a darkness that offered no shelter, its hideous, delayed end at the hands of a man it had not harmed in any way. I wanted to belabour Louisa with a broom, smack the self-satisfaction right off her smug face and squash it flat with the nearest shovel. All I managed was a lecture about the sonar system of bats and a suggestion that she inform herself before persecuting a harmless animal and encouraging her children to adopt her own ridiculous beliefs.

What a weight of superstition some animals have to bear. At one time, a woman's accidental or shocking contact with animals during pregnancy routinely explained birthmarks or defects. Scapegoats were literally driven out, bearing the collective guilt. Witch hunters targeted the small animals kept as pets by lonely old women, calling them familiars, the devil in disguise. A bird in the house is a bad omen. Toads cause warts. Owls are wise. Black cats are unlucky, except in England, where they are encouraged to cross one's path. Bees have to be told when there's a death in the house. Snakes are slimy, but then, they are the root of all evil, at least in the Christian tradition, and have to carry the blame for Original

Sin, so it's no wonder that everybody avoids them. Animals—those lesser beings without the divine gift of reason, quite unable to answer back—are very convenient when we want to displace the responsibility for our misfortunes, or refuse to accept that any misfortune is merely the product of something as meaningless as chance.

Bats are in the same league as snakes when it comes to myth and superstition. The conviction that they will tangle themselves in people's hair is the mildest of the beliefs associated with them. Far more bizarre is the connection forged between bats, blood, and night. Bats are nocturnal; in colder climates they hide away in caves to hibernate; some feed on animal blood. That much is observable fact. The bloodsucking lends itself to lurid exaggerations about animals being sucked dry overnight, and from there it is an easy leap to the vampires of Eastern Europe, to the strange appetite for blood, to the clawed fingers of Nosferatu and the bat-like shadow of Dracula against the moon, rising from their coffins to take possession of the night, shunning the light of the sun and living forever.

This strange intertwining of dark fantasies has a powerful hold on our imaginations. We may be far better informed about bats nowadays: any number of parks and nature reserves hold workshops to educate the public about them; instructions for building bat houses are easy to find (though not so easy to implement; you have to lure new tenants by putting some bat droppings in the house); governments pass laws to protect the animals. In some parts of the world, in India, and South America, at the Carlsbad Caverns, New Mexico, and in Austin, Texas, bat colonies have become tourist attractions. Most people know that bats are worth far more than their weight in gold for insect control; not quite so many people know that the fruit-eating bats of the Amazon are the foremost vector in plant propagation. Still, their bad press haunts them. In our brains, right alongside all the facts about their usefulness, lurk the atavistic myths of blood and night. We can marvel at their echo-sounding techniques and their social structure, but we continue to include the bat in our Halloween decorations.

I loved the bats that lived over my kitchen door. I never tired of watching them on summer evenings, the ecstatic swooping launch in the twilight, the curious softness of their flight, the secret hint of darkness moving in the dark. It pleased me that they chose to live on my house; I listened to their sleepy chatter and smiled, grateful that they never tired of consuming mosquitoes and blackflies.

But I will not soon forget the nightmare face that crawled out of the wall and left me frozen at the top of my ladder, waiting for my heart to slow.

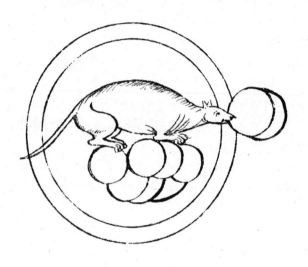

DOMINION

It must have been a slow news day for the story to appear on the front page. Or perhaps the report had stopped the editor in his tracks, much as the headline, below the fold but still prominent, arrested me.

"Blazing Mouse Sets Fire to House"

Admit it. You would have read on, too.

> "A US man who threw a mouse onto a pile of burning leaves could only watch in horror as it ran into his house and set the building ablaze."

The rest of the very brief story filled in the details. Eighty-one-year-old Luciano Mares, of Fort Sumner, New Mexico, had apparently caught the mouse in his house and "wanted to get rid of it." His own words capture the next steps: "I had some leaves burning outside, so I threw it in the fire, and the mouse was on fire and ran back at the house."

The house and everything in it was totally consumed by the flames.

The only comment came from the captain of the local fire department who allowed that in his experience—which was probably extensive since New Mexico was suffering from unseasonably dry and windy conditions at the time, during which well over 51,000 hectares had been devastated and ten homes destroyed by major blazes—the fire was unique.

That, it seems to me, is the least significant aspect of the story, though viewing the event simply as a firefighting anomaly is eloquent in its own way. The little report haunted me. I clipped the paragraph and kept reading it. Not once did I ponder the uniqueness of the fire.

Instead, I thought about the irresponsibility of one who burns leaves in a season of wildfires and drought. Surely at eighty-one he was old enough to know better? I puzzled over his approach to dealing with what he probably called vermin. If he wanted to kill the mouse, why didn't he use a trap? And if he went to the trouble of capturing it alive, why then did he throw it on the fire? Why not simply release it away from the house? And I contemplated the resultant horror, the cartoon-like sequence of cause and effect, and mused on karma, not quite able to resist the temptation of saying, "Serves you right."

For that eighty-one-year-old voice, quavery from shock and more than slightly aggrieved, sounds in my head: "I had some leaves burning outside, so I threw it in the fire . . ." It's the "so" that troubles me. What it says is that he was conveniently getting rid of garbage already and simply added a bit more. Presumably, if he had been operating a wood chipper at the time, that would have served exactly the same purpose. For him, the mouse—a living creature—had no more significance than the contents of the cat's litter box, or potato peelings, or the sweepings from the floor, no more significance even than a dead mouse. And if taxed with the monstrousness of his action, I have no doubt that he would protest, "But it was only a mouse!"

I confess to an affection for mice, albeit tempered with guilt. The very first pet I can remember was a white mouse with red eyes, called Ruby. My uncle, who must have been fifteen or sixteen at the time, had won her at a fair, and persuaded my mother that a mouse would be an ideal pet for me, especially as he would make her a cage. He did, too, in short order, and since he has always been very clever with his hands, as they say, the cage was a miniature palace for a rodent. It was a box with a sliding glass panel in the front, two floors connected by a ramp, and a hinged top held firm by a little brass hook. Ruby seemed to like it and soon settled in; my mother liked it because it was easy to keep clean; I liked it, and Ruby, because they were my very own.

Ruby was a revelation. She was so small, far smaller than me, yet she seemed fearless. This was probably because she was practically blind, like most albino creatures, and relied mostly on her senses of smell and hearing to alert her to danger. She would run up my arms and over my head, investigating all the folds in my clothing on the way. I would feel her restless whiskers in my ears and her smooth tail sliding round my neck as she rappelled down my chest. Everything about her fascinated me: her translucent ears, so delicate I could see all their threadlike veins; her tiny pink feet with their slivers of claws that you could feel but hardly see; the way she held her food in her front paws and nibbled with Lilliputian ivory teeth; her washing techniques, so like a cat's, but all the movements scaled down, speeded up, refined.

I loved Ruby, but this is where the guilt comes in, even though it was postdated by many years. Ruby liked her freedom, and returning her to her cage demanded quick reflexes to prevent her from making an escape before the lid could be fastened. On one occasion, I must have been quick, but not quite quick enough; my mother discovered Ruby dead, her neck trapped between the lid and the top of the glass wall. I do

not remember any of this; no doubt I was spared the trauma, and Ruby's body was whisked away to be disposed of somewhere—yes, probably into the garbage—and I was fed some story about her disappearance that satisfied me at the time. I didn't learn the truth until I was an adult.

Two dead mice, and the story of one must colour my reaction to the other to some extent. But am I overreacting to see that burning mouse as a symbol of a uniquely human trait: cruelty, and specifically, cruelty to animals?

Homo sapiens is an amazingly successful species. By rights, it should be impossible for such a puny creature to lord it at the top of the food chain. We are singularly ill-equipped for personal survival: no teeth or claws worth a damn, no fur, no tough hide, no scales, no venom, no camouflage, no offensive smell to make enemies reel back, gagging. We are slow, inept at climbing or tunnelling, sensitive to heat and cold. By comparison with most mammals, we have a pathetic sense of smell. We cannot hear as well as our dogs and cats. The octopus has a better-designed eye; spiders have a more refined sense of touch. We can reproduce at will, but our offspring are vulnerable for years. We should, in fact, be sitting ducks for every predator, extinct long since, an aberrant hiccup on the evolutionary path.

Instead, our highly evolved brains have circumvented our deficiencies and allowed us to flourish. We crowd the earth, muscling in and elbowing aside, because we can. Tigers do not form opposition parties when their jungle habitat falls to chainsaws; whales do not blockade ports and sewage outfalls; no polar bears mount rallies to protest global warming. Instead, they quietly decline, and leave us to our supremacy.

In that undisputed ascendancy lies the clue, I think, to our bent for cruelty. Any act of cruelty, on any scale, from schoolyard torments to mass murder, is a demonstration of power. Human beings have a sophisticated repertoire and an impressive history in the unspeakable, and every example one might summon up—female circumcision, torture—springs from a lust for control.

That we do these things to one another is appalling, but explicable. Life is a struggle after all, and life at the top is traditionally precarious, so a measure of ruthlessness may be expected, especially when that highly evolved brain can devise any number of religions or ideologies or cultures or paranoias to justify such behaviour. To be fair, right-minded people everywhere abhor cruelty; it is one of the few taboos left, and those guilty of it are reviled and even sometimes punished (often by methods that deserve their own chapter in the annals of inhumanity, but that is another issue). If it simply involved humans being cruel to other humans, we might sigh and accept it as an unfortunate quirk in an otherwise exceptional creature.

That is not the case, however. The Mengeles and the Dahmers—the monsters—form a grotesque pantheon of perversion, yet their celebrity status is due at least partly to their comparative rarity. Most people shudder at the very thought of such excesses. Yet there are hundreds, thousands, of otherwise unremarkable men and women who might never lay a hand on a fellow human, but who think nothing of abusing an animal.

Just over two years ago, my husband, Alan, decided he would like a dog. He had a yen for a basset hound. Always the efficient researcher, he surfed the Net for information about the breed and the location of breeders, and gave me daily bulletins on the results of his browsing. At first he was set on having a puppy, and actually found a breeder who could supply one, but the price was somewhat daunting. Plan B was adoption, so he started looking for Basset Rescues, and that is when the whole tenor of the search changed. Animal shelters habitually provide biographies of the animals they are offering for adoption on their websites, and a sorry litany it is.

We read about bassets found wandering alone along roads, their pads raw and bleeding; unwanted bassets thrown out of moving cars in supermarket parking lots; females used as puppy machines until they were exhausted, their abdominal muscles ruined; one, in Texas, whose ears were cut off.

Such histories are commonplace on the numerous rescue websites, but there is no need to go to the trouble of searching the Internet for them; similar reports abound in the press and on the air. In the short time we have lived on Vancouver Island we have heard a number of horror stories: dozens of dogs seized, found penned in barns up to their bellies in their own waste; ostriches deliberately driven from their pens at night by intruders to fall victim to passing cars; a pregnant rabbit hung up by the neck and used as a punching bag.

Why do the individuals responsible feel they have the right to inflict such suffering on creatures dependent on them, or quietly going about their lives, minding their own business? Strip away the rationalizations—drunkenness, ignorance, laziness, a totally misplaced sense of fun—and what is left is the same miserable demonstration of power, only this time on the part of those who, one suspects, have no other way to feel in control of anything. They see their victims as inferior to themselves: "just animals," not subject to the same considerations and respect as humans. Interesting that the perpetrators of the most inhuman savageries against fellow humans—the Holocaust, for example, the genocides in Rwanda and Darfur, apartheid in South Africa—have used exactly the same argument.

The Afrikaaners turned to their Bibles to justify their oppression of the coloured majority, and the same book may well have influenced the tendency to regard animals as expendable inferiors. Here is verse twenty-six of the first chapter of Genesis: "And God said, Let us make man in our own image after our likeness and let them have dominion over the fish of the sea, and over the fowl of the air, and over the cattle, and over all the earth, and over every creeping thing that creepeth upon the earth."

And two verses later, after God has created man (and woman), he sends them out with this instruction: "Be fruitful, and multiply, and replenish the earth, and subdue it: and have dominion over the fish of the sea, and over the fowl of the air, and over every living thing that moveth upon the earth."

Notice those words: "dominion" and "subdue." There it is: power and control. Bearing in mind how influential the Bible has been on Western culture, it is not surprising that the mindset it encouraged should still be embedded, even though few people have an intimate knowledge of the text nowadays. While Mr. Mares and his throwaway mouse shock us, they shouldn't surprise us. Plenty of those people whose animals have been seized protest bitterly about the invasion of their privacy and demand the return of their victims; at least one, recently, made exactly

that fuss when his sixty husky-cross dogs were rescued from conditions that sickened experienced officers, even though he had been charged with and convicted of similar offences in the past. The sense of entitlement is deeply entrenched.

Alan drew my attention to a cartoon in the paper. The first frame shows a man in an easy chair in front of his television, his dog asleep on a rug at his side. He is watching the news. To his increasing discomfort in succeeding frames, the announcer says, "Police raided a puppy mill, liberating twenty-five diseased and starving dogs. A dog was discovered chained to a tree, her collar so tight, it was cutting into her skin. An injured dog was found in a trash can, abandoned by his owner." The last frame has the man hugging his bewildered dog in a close embrace, saying, "I apologize for the behaviour of some humans," while a big question mark hovers in the dog's thought bubble.

The mouse now has a permanent place in the ragbag of my thoughts. I see it in my mind's eye, snatched up and tossed, not maliciously but, even worse, indifferently, into the searing heat of the bonfire. I see its panicked scramble to escape the flaring leaves, its whiskers burned off, fur alight, the hairs crackling and curling, tiny paws blistering, the tender skin of its ears turning black as it races back to the only shelter it has ever known, collapsing finally under the floorboards, in the wall or on a rug, somewhere, and the hungry flames moving on, further and further, unsatisfied.

It is no longer just a mouse, if, indeed, it ever was. It represents every animal victim of human cruelty and arrogance, every bear murdered for its gall bladder, every small dog stolen and thrown to pit bulls to teach them to kill, every living lobster lowered into a pot of boiling water. There is only one thing to say to the whole ghastly parade of the cowed and neglected, the starved and abused.

I apologize for the behaviour of some of my kind.

SENTENCED TO LIFE

I had rarely been so close to any bird of prey, let alone eagles. We were halfway through our lightning trek from Shanghai to Beijing in 1989, some forty or so students from a number of secondary schools in the Interior of British Columbia, accompanied by fifteen adults, teachers, administrators, and spouses on an educational trip subsidized by the British Columbia government in the first flush of its hands-across-the-ocean enthusiasm for Pacific Rim rapprochement. We were supposed to be ambassadors of a sort, sent to gain some familiarity with a culture that had been resolutely closed for so long, to learn what we could in two weeks, to soak up impressions freely like so many thirsty sponges. In reality, we were the sheltered wards of the Chinese government, herded to approved sites by friendly border collies masquerading as official tour guides. Under our bemused gaze, the collective farm drowning in rain succeeded the Jade Buddha Temple, the Ming tombs followed the language school, the silk factory gave way to the Great Wall. These carefully orchestrated twitchings of the curtain *were* informative—not always, I suspect, in the ways our hosts intended—but we sponges were quickly supersaturated. Nothing can adequately prepare Westerners for the sensory overload of China; that first welter of impressions takes months to process.

I often wonder why the zoo was on the itinerary. What did the Chinese think we would take away from it? Was it merely a diversion, a sop for our unserious Western minds? Something entertaining for the children? Whatever the intent, I am sure my reaction would have caused dismay in the hearts of the bureaucrats in the Ministry of Tourism.

Our bus drew up outside a park. It contained a zoo, they told us. There was a huge sign at the entrance: a dragon with a large pearl in its mouth—power with wisdom. Chinese dragons are benign, not malevolent; they are creatures of water, not fire; they protect, they don't destroy. Already our visit was heavy with symbolism, and we hadn't even gone through the gates yet. The irony came later.

The park was pleasant enough, but it was immediately obvious that the facilities were not on the cutting edge of zoo design. There was a huddle of antique cages, cramped barred boxes with dirty concrete floors. They reminded me of rare visits to London Zoo when I was a child, the solid Victorian ironwork, the shadowy cells where animals blinked in the gloom, black bars striping the hopeless indolence. Perhaps my brain immediately threw up a defensive wall, because I remember little of the animals in that Chinese park apart from the occupants of two cages.

In one, a lone panda slumped dejectedly in its stall. Its fur was dirty and so was its cage. It did not appear to have any food, and it was thousands of miles from the bamboo forests of its birth.

This was bad enough—the iconic animal so neglected, so dingy and depressed—but the other cage haunts me still, the trigger of such consuming anger, such pity, that it is indelible. It stood near the lake, a cast-iron version of the bamboo cages the Chinese use to house their beloved linnets and finches and canaries, a whimsical, circular, gazebo-like structure that could easily serve as a summer house or small bandstand.

It housed three huge eagles. They perched on three metal hoops arranged in a ring around the centre of the cage.

They had the fierce gaze of their kind; their tawny eyes took us in and dismissed us, returned to their distant contemplation. Their feathers were brown, with infinitely subtle variations and gradations of brown-ness like the bark of trees.

Everything about them spelled power: the cruel curve of the beaks, the brooding hunch of the shoulders, the wedges of tail feathers, the weaponry of legs and talons. But they were warrior kings brought low, whiling away their captivity with ineffectual memories of greatness.

Their wingspan was immense, at least six feet and probably more. Their cage was small, the perches close together. When they unfurled their wings, they jostled one another, and the cage looked as if it had suddenly filled with drying umbrellas.

All three faced into the brisk wind coming off the water. They stretched their vast wings and, as they sensed the lift, they made brief hops into the air, for a few seconds resting on the invisible currents, riding the atmosphere, the great drifting spiral a wingbeat away, until the roof of the cage intervened and pressed them back onto their perches once more.

That was the moment, I think, when I ceased being ambivalent about zoos. For most of my life to that time, zoos were a guilty pleasure. They fed my passion for animals, my fascination with the immense variety of living things, with the mind-blowing ingenuity of their evolution and the elegance of their adaptation to their environments. They allowed me to see exotic species whose countries of origin I would probably never visit; I could come close enough to smell their wildness, to look them in the eye and catch a glimpse of alien ways of looking at the world. I could watch seals close their nostrils and rocket their bulk through the water; stand beside a somnolent tiger, listening to it purr; marvel as snakes convulsed out of their skins, to emerge freshly painted beside the ghost of their old selves.

But while one part of my mind was relishing these delights, another was compiling a different sort of list. The seals look as if they're having fun, said analytical brain, but isn't their pool awfully small? Why is that chimpanzee rocking backwards and forward? Doesn't it remind you of pictures you've seen of the mentally ill? What kind of life is it for an elephant, born to wander for years across hundreds of miles of savannah, to be chained by one ankle to a stake in the middle of a paddock?

One of my very earliest zoo memories symbolizes all this unease. As a child, I lived near Chessington Zoo, southwest of London. Going there was an occasional treat; it had a fun fair as well as animals, and provided a reasonable day's entertainment for families. The thing that remains with me about the place, apart from the memory of a bad case of sunstroke after one visit, is the polar bear. At that time (it's quite different now) there was just one hapless specimen. He was housed behind bars in a space approximately fifteen feet long by eight feet wide. There was a trough in the centre of the cage, somewhat larger than a regulation bathtub, but not much, filled with water of an unlovely cloudy green. The bear paced incessantly in an unvarying pattern: up one side of the cage, pause in the corner to swing his head from side to side three times, back the length of the cage to swing his head in the other corner, turn, down the length of the cage, swing three times, back, swing three times . . .

Did he dream of ice beneath his feet? Of swimming from floe to floe? Of the scent of seals? Of the long dark and the never-sleeping sun? Or worse, was there nothing for him but the stench of the rank water and the dead fish he was fed and his own waste, too much heat, too much boredom, nothing but endurance and madness?

Of course, zoos have come a long way from that time, when they were not much more than glorified freak shows. The public is more knowledgeable, more aware of the nature and needs of the animals, largely thanks to all those animal documentaries on television bringing, right into people's living rooms, lions hunting wildebeest, cheetahs dragging antelopes up trees, crocodiles attacking their prey, and lyre birds embellishing their nests.

Nowadays, zoos have to satisfy their patrons that the animals' lives are as pleasant as possible. The more creative ones have concentrated on providing habitats that closely simulate the animals' native homes, and on finding sources of natural food or evolving substitutes that measure up nutritionally. You will find clever displays of nocturnal creatures, such as bats, specially lit so that the animals think it is night in the middle of the day and the public can clearly see their behaviour. Many zoos, the earliest being Whipsnade just after the Second World War, provide huge paddocks, convincing savannahs and grasslands where herd animals, big cats, elephants, giraffe, kangaroos, rhinoceros, hyenas, and wild dogs can wander and hide. There have been amazingly ingenious attempts to show birds at their best, like the huge aviary designed by Lord Snowdon for London Zoo, an airy construct of very high poles and netting built around mature trees, in which the birds are free to fly and nest and feed, and the humans are the ones constrained.

That seems to be the secret of the modern zoo. It is the animals' well-being that comes first now; to see the creatures, humans walk among them in tunnels or on glassed-in paths, or ride the grasslands in special trains or vehicles: close but separate. I came across one of the best examples of this kind of ingenuity in Southern California in the mid-1980s.

I remember standing in the enormous warehouse that San Diego's Sea World had just converted into a habitat for their penguins, gliding slowly on the moving walkway past the teeming marine life beyond the floor-to-ceiling glass, and thinking, *This* is how zoos ought to be.

The ice gleamed, pure notes of aquamarine and emerald in its depths. The water was jade, and crystalline. There were shelves of rough black rock, mounds of snow. Seabirds soared and dived. Penguins big and small, of every kind, filled the eye. They stood and shuffled like glum underemployed waiters with sore feet. They tumbled and slid down ice shelves into the water, transformed instantly from clowns into superathletes, flying underwater at breakneck speed, sleek black torpedoes that hurtled back to shore, popping out of the water again like champagne corks. They waved their stubby wings at each other, clacked beaks, bickered and preened. Some lay flat on their chests and pushed themselves along the ice like miniature Olympians at the top of a luge run.

And they talked. The rasping babble of their conversations filled the huge space, the deafening, ceaseless noise of hundreds of strange birds, familiar to us from television documentaries, but here in real time, a monstrous, unlikely slice of Antarctic life transplanted whole into the California sun.

It was a far cry from the soupy green ponds and fouled concrete ramps most zoo penguins have to call home. The birds themselves were different, too, quite unlike the dispirited creatures we have all seen, their feathers a dull grey as if they have been washed too many times in a shabby laundromat, standing motionless for so long that visitors hanging over the railings, willing them to dive, twitch, open a beak, lift a wing, blink—anything that might betray a spark of animation—grow bored and move on to the sleeping lions.

Obviously, the faux Antarctica is preferable to the soupy pond if you're going to keep wild animals in captivity, although it's a hard ideal to realize: I've no doubt the refrigeration costs alone are prohibitive for Sea World. I'm perfectly aware that a good case can be made for collecting animals for people to see: it is educational; it makes people aware of the diversity of life on the planet; it encourages ecological sensitivity. There is no question, either, that some zoos, responsive to ecological move-ments and the terrifying impact of human development on the planet's flora and fauna, are doing sterling work safeguarding endangered species with breeding programs. The California condor, for example, pretty well extinct in the wild, has been brought back from the abyss at the San Diego Zoo, the condor chicks fed by attendants wearing large glove puppet condor heads on their arms so that they are never habituated to human contact.

But do you notice how often I have used words and phrases like "simulate," "faux," "as pleasant as possible?" However thrilling a zoo is, however worthy its aims and convincing its habitats, no matter how excellent its care, it is artificial. No animal would choose to live in one. Wild animals are dangerous, so they have to be contained, and however humane and generous the accommodation, zoos are unnatural prisons.

Cruel and unusual punishment certainly comes to mind when I think of those eagles in China. What a terrible fate for such noble creatures, deprived of their lordly mastery of the air, great predators at the top of their food chain reduced to scraps in begging bowls, their only pleasure a ghostly whisper of the joy of flight. And what an indictment of the men who stole their freedom and sentenced them to life imprisonment for no other crime than their rarity and beauty, for no rational purpose except to show that they could.

MERLIN

My garden froze. Nothing to do with temperature. At the time, I was lolling on the deck behind my house, enjoying an idle hour on a perfect day in early fall. The poplar leaves were turning yellow, not yet the luminous gold that makes the trees seem lit from within at twilight, but a bravura contrast to the cloudless sky. They shivered helplessly in the still air, rustling, and the thread of sound was as soothing as running water.

The grass—lawn would hardly be an accurate word for what was more like a hayfield regularly shorn—surrounded the house like a moat, and stopped short at a tumbledown fence that marked the boundary of the cleared area of the property. The bush bellied up to the other side of the fence, contemplating invasion. When we first moved in, that area had been clear of underbrush, thanks to the restless feet of the previous owners' sled dogs, but now the vegetation had grown over and it was impossible to see far into the trees.

Birds loved it. I kept my feeders in the trees along the fence line and spent hours watching the visitors. That morning flocks of juncos scoured the ground for fallen seed, scuffling in the dead leaves; there were so many small brown bodies and black heads joining the search that the earth seethed. Chickadees and purple finches flitted amongst the branches, cheerfully garrulous, and a solitary nuthatch sidled down the trunk of the cottonwood. A pileated woodpecker swooped between trees, looping up great swathes of air and hammering them fast to the bark. All were so busy and intent, and the air so full of their voices—cheeping, rasping, calling—the purring of their wings, the tiny scratchings of their feet and beaks, that my lids drooped.

Then silence.

My eyes, prompted by who-knows-what atavistic fear, flew open. Just in time. A shadow slalomed through the trees and on a gasp, hundreds of wings clapped thunderously as one and disappeared like buckshot, sucked into limbo, except for one small brown finch impaled in mid-flight. Without a pause the slender wings and strong barred tail tilted and flirted, and the merlin was gone.

The silence held. I could see a little downy woodpecker glued to a tree trunk. A few tiny brown feathers were still drifting down. Nothing else moved.

I timed it. Fifteen minutes went by before the woodpecker shifted. Immediately, I heard the first inquiring cheep from a chickadee and the trees seemed to breathe again. Soon after that, the juncos returned and once more went to work on the seeds pushed out of the feeders.

I was left to marvel: at the fear that one relatively small creature could inspire; at the skill of the predator, negotiating the trees at high speed and picking off one diminutive victim out of a cloud of frightened birds scattering to every point of the compass; at the phlegmatic return of the survivors, picking up where they had left off, until the next time the merlin went hunting; at my luck in being there to see something that happens all the time, but rarely in front of witnesses.

Not that we were unaware of the merlin's presence. We saw it frequently, admired its rapid, straight flight, the neat rake of its wings. My husband had even been privy to another guerrilla raid, which had left him gasping: he had been standing by one of our apple trees, inspecting it for signs of actual fruit (not a foregone conclusion in northern British Columbia), when the merlin snatched one of the ubiquitous chickadees out of the air literally in front of his nose.

Nor was it the only predator around. Eagles and ospreys abounded; the calls of owls and foxes kept me awake at night. There were plenty of mink and weasels, martens and otters, bears and cougars, even wolves—more than enough predators, in fact, to make the preyed-upon permanently watchful.

I find it hard to imagine that level of fear and the built-in resignation that accepts the likelihood of becoming some other creature's lunch as a normal part of life. We are fortunate, I suppose, that, except for rare instances, we are not regarded as prey. On those occasions when it does happen—when a shark attacks a swimmer, when a grizzly bear drags off a camper, when a cougar ambushes a child straggling behind a group of hikers—the anxiety level instantly peaks, and all efforts aim at finding and eliminating the culprit, often an injured or immature, hungry animal whose need has compelled it to approach humans.

For the remarkable thing about predators is their restraint. Their motive is simply to find something to eat when they are hungry, not to indulge blood lust. That they leave to the worst predator of all.

According to scientists it is humans' evolved brain that has made predators of us. It made us successful, ensured that we dreamed up ways to protect ourselves in spite of our vulnerability, allowed us to become so prolific that we dominate the Earth and bend other species to our will, battening on them in a way no other creature has ever considered. We carry predation to quite another level without ever once thinking of ourselves as predators, and restraint has never been our middle name.

Take our food, for instance. We have to eat, obviously, and we are omnivores; we cannot be faulted for consuming the occasional pork chop or chicken breast. But did we have to invent factory farming: huge numbers of pigs and chickens kept in barracks because it's more convenient that way, never seeing the light of day? Clever of somebody to come up with pâté, but did we have to nail the feet of geese to a board and force-feed them until their livers were diseased in order to make it extra rich? Fish is delicious, but only humans would construct nets so long and deep that they catch everything in their path, edible or not. Only humans, I'm afraid, would sever the fins of sharks and dump the victims overboard to die, just to make soup.

Our predatory footprints show up everywhere. You will find them around the bodies of elephants slaughtered for their tusks; in the severed bear paws and dreadful gobbets of bloody flesh I saw for sale on the Bund in Shanghai; in the clear-cuts in the Amazon that endanger hundreds of species, some not even yet known. We tear up the Earth for its wealth; we pollute water and air. We know we are changing the climate of the planet but we seem unable or unwilling to stop. There is no restraint in any of this.

And we have taken predation even further. Few animals, unless stressed beyond endurance, make a habit of turning on their own kind. We do. We fight wars; we invent excuses to demonize those who are different and make their lives a torment; we set out to murder entire races. This we do on a grand scale, at national or global levels, and at a more local level, with gangs, muggings and assaults, street racing, home invasions and all the sordid, sorry dealings of the drug trade.

Although we are reluctant to see the human race in this light, we do recognize some particularly odious criminal activities as predatory, and we label stalkers and pedophiles and serial killers as dangerous predators, beyond the pale. At the same time, we have evolved a wonderful new playground for those with a taste for hunting and trapping human victims: we call it the Internet and fail completely to make it safe, even while we allow it to grow exponentially.

This behaviour is a far cry from the innocence of that random intersection of the flight of two birds. One finch died and the merlin eased its hunger; dozens of small birds were safe to go about their business for another day. There is no malice in that, no wanton destruction for its own sake; above all no greed. In its own way, it has a certain grace and beauty.

Not so long ago I was walking down Fort Street in Victoria and came upon a little knot of people standing on the sidewalk where an alley between buildings opened onto the street. They were all staring into the alley, so I joined them to see what they were looking at so intently. About ten feet away stood a young peregrine falcon, unhurriedly tearing strips of flesh from the pigeon it had just killed. Some of the people watching turned away, making sounds of disgust and revulsion; some laughed. Most, though, watched quietly. They made no move to shoo the raptor away, or deprive it of its meal. There was an almost reverent stillness, as if they had stumbled inadvertently upon the celebration of a sacrament, deeply meaningful, among the dumpsters and the grimy litter of the alleyway, with the unheeding traffic hissing and blaring behind them.

And they were right, for it was a sign of the natural order that we seem determined to derange. All around us the natural predators roam: owls float soundless in the moonlight on their specially designed wing feathers; pike glide up on unsuspecting fish at the bottom of lakes; jewel-like dragonflies terrorize the insect populations over ponds; spiders weave their gleaming traps in hedges. It is the way of the world, left to its own devices, and because the prey almost always vastly outnumber the predators, who never take more than they need to survive and raise their young, the result is balance. Only human beings give predation a bad name; the merlin and the peregrine simply earn our respect as perfect hunters who know only the direct path, and freeze the heart's core with intimations of mortality.

One last note. Not long after the merlin silenced my garden, I found its limp body near my house. Deceived by open vistas and distant trees, it had smashed into one of our windows and broken its neck.

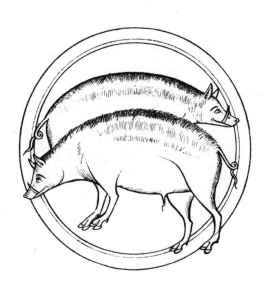

PIGS MIGHT FLY

I had an uncle who looked just like a pig. Surviving photographs— dignified under mayoral chains of office, younger and jauntier in First World War uniform—confirm that this was not just a child's impression. The head is massive, Churchillian, sunk into the shoulders like a cannonball on a mound of dough. The face is round and scraped pink (in memory, not in the photographs) and there are jowls, plump and smooth. The features crowd rather into the middle: small eyes behind spectacles with tiny round lenses; a snub nose offering a rather clearer view of the nostrils than is usual; a generous mouth, thick-lipped. Later, when I read the scene at the end of *Animal Farm*, in which the animals staring through the farmhouse window are no longer able to tell the difference between the pigs and the men, it was Uncle Horace with trotters who leaped into my mind.

There was a rightness to this resemblance, a magical confluence of form and purpose. For my uncle was a butcher, and not just any old butcher, but a pork butcher, a specialist common at that time, in East Anglia at least, but now nowhere to be found. He sold other meats, too, for faithful customers who wanted a change, but pork dominated.

I'd watch him in his shop, binding boneless loins with neat flicks of the string; filling the gleaming trays with chops and grey peppery sausages (the best I've ever, ever eaten); wrapping the shiny brown pork pies in greaseproof paper; carving thick slices of pink-grey salt pork; scoring the rind on a roast so that it would make a diamond pattern of delicious crackling when it was cooked.

There was more to this connection. My uncle did not simply sell meat. He was a farmer, too, and raised pigs for his shop. At weekends, or on summer evenings, he would drive out to the farm and wade into the wheat field to pick a sample ear and roll the seeds between thumb and forefinger in a knowledgeable way, or lean against the pigsty, talking to Joe, the Italian ex-POW who had elected to stay in England after the war and continue to look after the farm. I'd listen to the enquiring grunts from the adult pigs, and think how like them my uncle was. He, too, even in the house, communicated in what sounded like a series of grunts and bass mumbles, unintelligible to my ear, but which my aunt could interpret and answer from several rooms away.

There was a similar level of communication between the other pigs that populated my childhood and the man who looked after them. My father worked for a wholesale seed firm which had trial grounds in Colchester, large fields where samples of the seeds in the firm's catalogue were tried out. My father would go there to check on germination rates, quality of produce and seed, and the purity of the stock, counting the "rogues"—the number of red wallflowers in a row of yellow, for instance, or the intruding Pheasant's Eye narcissus in a planting of King Alfred daffodils. For some reason, the farm was also home to a very big herd of pedigree Large White pigs, and any visit to the trial grounds without seeing them was incomplete.

They lived in a big complex of immaculate sties. Each sow had a pen to herself, and many of them would have gaggles of scampering, squealing piglets. The sties were always noisy, but when the pigs realized that Mr. Firmin was bringing visitors around, there would be an instant alert: pigs lumbering to their feet, the wet rubbery disks of their snouts tilting and flexing, their heads pushed against the gates, eyes squinched half-shut in ecstasy as a hand scratched the solid necks just behind their flopping ears. The man always seemed to know how each pig felt: which ones were off-colour, which were sad, which were likely to turn on their young. He claimed to know what they said as they snorted and squealed, and I saw no reason to doubt him. It was quite obvious to me, from the knowing, twinkly look in their tiny eyes, that these were sociable animals with far more brain power than, say, cows; of course they responded to kindness, and enjoyed the communication through sound and body language.

Not that I did much thinking along these lines at the time. Then, I simply enjoyed them as something far outside the ordinary confines of my life. I loved their bulk, their pink skin shining through the scattering of coarse white hair, their canny expressions, their prissy feet that reminded me irresistibly of overweight ladies wearing unsuitable high heels. I loved the way they lay like beached whales on their sides while their babies lined up in military order to suckle. Above all, I loved their complete abandon in the presence of food, their hysterical shrieking as they smelt its approach, and the way the bedlam diminished, sty by sty, as the mash was poured into the troughs and splashed over the snouts and feet of the impatient animals, to a final contented undertone of slobbering, slurping, smacking relish.

And then there was the boar.

He was a creature of mythical proportions. Since these were pedigree pigs, and it was a breeding herd, the boar had an almost sacred importance. As with many valuable stud animals, his likes and dislikes were observed, his moods studied; he had a reputation for unpredictability, cruel and kind on a whim, rather like a farmyard Nero. I was expressly forbidden to approach him on my own.

He lived alone on the other side of the yard in a large building with a Dutch door. The upper half of the door was invariably open, but I was too short to peer over the bottom half; to see anything, I had to stand on an upturned bucket.

First, my eyes had to adjust to the darkness inside, and while they were doing that, my nose would twitch at the warm smell of dust, of manure, of some large living presence, and there would be sounds: rasping breath, stirrings in slippery straw. And then, an immense shadowy bulk would lurch out of the gloom, a Zeppelin of a pig, emitting low snuffling grunts in a profound bass with every laboured step he took toward the light and a rare audience with his subjects.

He inspired awe. I was used to big animals; I had no fear of my uncle's great Suffolk Punch horses, for instance, just a step down from Clydesdales, and quite as gentle. But I had no wish to approach the boar. He was quiet with Mr. Firmin scratching the slab of his back with a hard broom, but he was too massive, there was too much force pent up in that bulk, he was too far removed from the cozy squealing world of the piglets across the yard. He seemed a creature of mysteries, as strange and exalted and incalculable in his gloomy solitude as the Sibyl herself.

But he was an exceptional animal. Insulated from the grim world of factory farming, most humans unconsciously sustain a comfortable, jokey relationship with pigs, almost as if the animals are slovenly, undisciplined younger siblings whose behaviour alternately disgusts and amuses us but who are tolerated because they are part of the clan and, underneath all that squalor, might actually have something going on in their heads.

Let someone cram his mouth with food, chew with his mouth open, spill gravy down his clothes, hunch over his plate with his elbows on the table, deprive others with his greed, and we call him a "pig." Abandon housework, let the dishes pile up in the sink, the dust bunnies under the bed, let the dirty washing overflow the laundry basket and the bathroom repel all boarders, and you have created a "pigsty." Yet it is hard to think of a disagreeable pig in any form of fiction, apart from the denizens of *Animal Farm*. Porky Pig, the Three Little Pigs, the Duchess of Blandings, Wilbur, Babe—all are charming in their separate ways, amusing and certainly unthreatening. Sir Winston Churchill probably spoke for many people when he said, "I like pigs. Dogs look up to us. Cats look down on us. Pigs treat us as equals."

Over large portions of the globe, pigs are the commonest domestic animal, apart from fowl. They live close to their owners, right in their houses in some cases, and are a staple form of sustenance and wealth. Even Westerners cuddle up to their pigs; Vietnamese pot-bellied pigs had the misfortune to become a trendy pet at one time, and dented the hardwood floors and graced the sofas of many a home, only to be abandoned when they became too much trouble—a disaster for a long-lived animal, and a problem for animal shelters. In recent floods in the Fraser Valley, one woman who was running an animal rescue on her property had to take extraordinary steps to look after her charges when her sheds were under three feet of water. She had nearly thirty pot-bellied pigs in her house—in the kitchen, in the sitting room, in the bathroom, and one "senior pig" in a special box wedged into a corner of the hallway between front door and kitchen, sheltered from the five or six other less privileged animals confined to the narrow space.

Obviously that woman felt there was something about pigs that demanded special treatment, and it is the same with other people I have seen or read about who keep pigs as house pets. Accompanying the photographs of pigs watching television, sitting between their owners on the sofa, or playing with the family dog, there are always the same comments: "He's so loving, so much fun, such good company, so clean—so *smart!*"

It's this last which perhaps gives one clue to that rather odd feeling of kinship. We like animals with intelligence, as long as they are not menacing, because they mirror to some extent, and flatter, our own cognitive superiority. I remember a colleague who used to dine out on his pig's exploits, notably the time the animal learned how to open the door of his dilapidated truck and took over the vehicle, using the front seat as a bed. He milked the situation for laughs, yet clearly he was proud of the pig's initiative. But I think about my uncle's uncanny resemblance to the animals he raised and sold, and wonder if there isn't also a link of an altogether more atavistic kind, hidden deep down on a cellular level.

For it's the pig's bad luck to have a certain level of compatibility with human organs; with the help of pigs, xenotransplantation moves out of the realm of science fiction and into everyday reality. My brother-in-law has a heart valve that used to belong to a pig. When I first heard about it, I gaped in disbelief. But blood flows through a pig's heart in the same way as a human's and such replacements have become common. They last on average about fifteen years, so they are usually the replacement of choice for older patients, and have the great advantage that they do not demand a lifetime regimen of anticoagulants.

Insulin is produced from pigs, and pig spleens have been used in an experimental treatment for diabetics which aims at creating new insulin-producing cells in the body so that injections are unnecessary or greatly curtailed. The skin of pigs has also been used for grafts on burn victims.

There are ethical concerns, of course, and problematical issues of animal diseases jumping the species barrier and mutating into forms lethal to humans, capable of resisting any known antidotes and causing pandemics. There have been warnings: mad cow disease, bird flu, and the recent outbreak of the H1N1 Influenza Virus, popularly known as Swine Flu, all underline the risk. Pigs carry the porcine endogenous retrovirus—charmingly termed PERV for short. It has never been known to cause disease in humans, but there could always be a first time; maybe the sheer possibility will be enough to postpone any wholesale trade in pig parts to offset the chronic shortage of human organs for transplant.

The business exists, though; there are farms in Australia that breed special small pigs whose heart valves are exactly the right size for humans, and to circumvent the threat of PERV, there is even a herd of pigs on a small uninhabited island between New Zealand and Antarctica which has been isolated ever since the animals were abandoned many years ago by explorers. They are completely disease-free: a medical research scientist's dream come true.

The truth is, the very qualities that have made pigs desirable companions over thousands of years of domestication—their social natures, their compatibility, their fertility, their sheer numbers in the world—have doomed them to something rather like the clones developed for spare parts predicted in Ishiguro's *Never Let Me Go*: nice creatures, but expendable when the time comes.

Nor does it stop there. The pig's physiological similarity to the human has made him a natural subject for another kind of experimentation, born of the terrible demands of warfare. Recently I heard someone on the radio describing how the armed services are evolving the most efficient ways of keeping severely injured soldiers alive long enough to reach more sophisticated medical assistance than can be found on the battlefield: specifically, to allay the effects of shock. This is difficult to assess with actual patients, and, as it is impossible to subject human guinea pigs to sufficient trauma to make the experiment realistic, the chosen subjects were pigs. Each paramedic had a pig; the task was to keep it alive for as long as possible. An officer inflicted catastrophic injuries on the animals, and the paramedics went to work on their patients, stabilizing them by any means possible. Then the pigs were injured again, multiple gunshot wounds from automatic weapons, shotgun blasts to the face, and stabilized again. The "winner" lasted fifteen hours.

I suppose I would welcome a xenotransplant if that were the only option. I accept that every day, people's lives are saved or improved by treatments that would have been impossible without the sacrifice of animals in one way or another. I might well be grateful that paramedics had amazing skills up their sleeves if I had a loved one on the front line, though I might also question the need for a front line and such trauma research in the first place.

It is hard on the pigs, though. Quite apart from making an acute observation on the nature of Fascism and Communism, and the essential corruption of power, George Orwell hit the nail on the head in *Animal Farm* when he made the ringleaders of the animals' revolt the pigs. Napoleon and Snowball and their henchmen are clever (though not infallible); there is always the sense that these are animals with potential, capable of evolving and adapting, capable of scaling the heights. Of course they represent humans in the story, and are therefore deeply flawed, but I have always felt that pigs could, if the evolutionary paths had taken slightly different routes, have aspired to greatness, and not just literally, in mammoth weight and size.

I prefer to use my uncle's pigs and the Large Whites of my childhood as my porcine benchmark. At least they seemed happy. It's not so easy to find contented barnyard pigs nowadays, but there's a little hobby farm quite close to my home where I can revive those memories. The farmer has five or six pigs, including a boar who lives with his harem in a large enclosure whose main feature is a mud wallow. They sleep side by side in a shed, according to a strict hierarchy, and coat themselves liberally with mud to ward off sunburn when it's hot. Everyone who lives nearby visits them to throw vegetable peelings over the single-strand electric fence that is all that's needed to keep them penned. I take them the windfall apples I can't deal with fast enough. They lumber out to snare the bouncing apples I've tossed into their pen, chewing their way methodically through pounds at a time.

I have a photograph of the old boar enjoying this feast. He is not your usual pig: dark brown and massive, he has huge tusks curving wickedly from his mouth. He is facing the camera, demolishing a large Gravenstein; his pink mouth is full of apple pieces, so many that some are spilling out, juice foaming down his jowls. I can still hear the crunching and sloshing, and see his eyes fixed ecstatically on a point just above my head, before he bends to retrieve the fallen crumbs and snorts after another apple, nipping one of his consorts sharply on the flank to push her away from his target. In the best of all possible pig worlds, that is a perfect moment.

GOAT

The flayed head lies in the refrigerated display case. It has a pared-down familiarity, much like the illustrations of musculature in anatomy textbooks. The eyes are dull stones and the jaw gapes a little, revealing worn yellow teeth. Where it was severed, the flesh has dried to a dull reddish brown; the ragged ends of bone stand out in contrast. The head rests on a pile of ribs; to one side there are other slabs of meat which could have been haunches, loins, shoulders. It has pride of place in the cabinet.

Alan and I have come on one of our leisurely shopping expeditions to the only supermarket in Koroni, a small fishing town in the Peloponnese. They are indolent affairs, partly because of the heat and the pleasure of idling in the air-conditioned store, and partly because time truly has little meaning apart from getting to the bakery just as the fresh batch of loaves comes out of the oven. So far I have collected cartons of apricot yoghurt, a jar of Nescafé and a packet of spaghetti.

Our wants are simple here. I have drifted by the butcher's section only to see if there is anything cheap I can use rather than canned meatballs, and to buy some of the feta cheese that the butcher hoists with a grappling hook out of a huge vat of brine.

The head stops us in our tracks. I'm not altogether sure what the animal is. Was. Sheep, perhaps? Goat?

We look at each other.

"What *is* that?" asks Alan. "You don't suppose . . . ?"

"No," I answer hurriedly. "No, it couldn't be, no."

But my protest sounds hollow even to my ears.

Summer had started just a few days earlier. After days of rain and unseasonal chill when we arrived at the campsite, the Greek spring had suddenly snapped out of depression and settled into cloudless skies, calm seas, and steadily rising temperatures. We were still the only people staying at Koroni Camping, and that afternoon we sat under the shifting silver shade of the olive trees and felt there could be no finer existence.

Out of sight, Anna, the owner of the campsite, was whitewashing the washrooms. I lounged, eyes closed against the glare, aware of nothing except the rise and fall of my own breathing and the susurration of small sounds around me. Cicadas shrilled, invisible, and grasshoppers clacked through skiffs of wildflowers. The brown crows chided each other in the tops of the trees, and a dog barked. Large, furry, blue bees droned past on a desultory breeze that smelled of sage and thyme and oregano, of hot dust and orange blossom and, faintly, of the delicate briny rot of the sea. And behind it all, the counterpoint of goats bleating to the dull clank of the bells hanging round their necks.

How Greek that sound is, I thought. How many times we've heard the flat plunking of the bells that heralded flocks of bearded goats moving fluidly down parched hillsides, across roads, accompanied by their herders, young boys waving long sticks and urging their charges on with staccato cries. And how often on our very first visit to Greece in the early 1960s we were faced with the fruits of their labours—cubes of dried goat cheese, so rank in flavour and smell that I was forced to slide them unobtrusively into my bag or pocket to avoid offending our hosts, because eating them was impossible. Months later, back in England, I would still find pungent crumbs to remind me of the goats, their strange eyes staring until they decided we were unworthy of attention.

My eyes opened. The bleating seemed louder. I could see the goats responsible for the sound. They were in an enclosure with a shed at one end, halfway up the steep hillside on the other side of the road. I watched them milling about for some time before I registered that their movements were restricted to one end of their paddock, and seemed agitated, as if the whole flock was anxious. And they were making a lot of noise.

At least, one of them was. My eye caught a spasmodic jerk right by the hut at the end of the enclosure fence. It happened again, and out of the mass of moving bodies, my attention fixed on one goat. But there was something odd about its shape. It looked as if it were reared up on its hind legs, standing full length against the building.

I fetched my binoculars. The goats on the hillside leaped into focus, so close that I could count them and describe their markings. But I was interested only in one.

To my horror I saw that the animal was not standing against the wall but hanging down. I felt a skip of apprehension.

"Oh no," I said. "Don't tell me it's going to be butchered."

As if to underline the possibility, the goat's helpless cries seemed even louder, now that I could see its mouth gaping and its sides heaving with every bleat and galvanic jerk. There were no people in sight, however, and no matter how callous the butcher, I could not imagine he would simply leave the goat hanging there until a convenient time.

"Let me see," said Alan, holding his hand out for the binoculars.

There was silence for a moment as he focused.

"No," he said, "I think it's caught on the fence. I bet it's tried to jump over."

Helplessly, we gazed at the animal far away up the hill, which our binoculars had brought too close to ignore. The situation demanded someone with local knowledge; we had no idea how to get to the goats, how to find their owner, or even how to talk to him when, and if, we found him. We needed Anna.

Alan found her hosing down the laundry, her rubber flip-flops slapping, hands encased in bright yellow industrial-strength rubber gloves, wet curls clinging to her face. She didn't understand "goat," but when we dragged her to see the animals, she nodded knowledgeably and said, "Yes, I see, sheep," only it sounded more like "ship."

"We go find," she said firmly, discarding her gloves.

Anna led us across the road, past the houses opposite until she came to a track leading into the trees. It rose steeply and we were soon puffing with exertion. At a point where the track widened and branched into two or three tributaries she told us to wait.

"Maybe I find the man with sheep," she said and disappeared.

We sat in the shade of a tree. The goats were nearby; the frantic bleating was much louder. By the time Anna trudged into view it had become intolerable.

"Nobody know who has sheep," said Anna, shrugging. "Not caring. We look."

Another scramble and we emerged suddenly into a clearing, and there was the back of the shed at the end of the enclosure. Some of the goats were distracted by our sudden appearance and clustered by the fence to stare, but we ignored them and hurried round the shed to the hapless victim.

A quick glance showed the full horror. The goat dangled from the fence, the whole weight of its oval body suspended by its right hind leg. It must have hurdled the wire, snagging that hoof in one of the holes, then tumbled to earth on the other side, snapping the bones above the hoof and folding the wire down over the foot, firmly trapping it.

We did what we could. Anna got into the enclosure through the shed, and while we wrestled the goat up, she pried the wire loose from the foot so that the animal could be bundled back over the fence. The goat was not co-operative. It bucked and struggled, its sharp hooves scrabbling for purchase against our arms and legs. Its mouth hung open and the tongue lolled; its eyes were blank with terror. We tried to free it without causing any additional suffering, but the awkwardness of its bulk and the intransigence of the wire conspired against us, and the need to get it done made us first clumsy, then desperate.

Finally, it was free. We dumped it unceremoniously into the enclosure and sighed with relief although we all knew we'd brought only temporary deliverance. Anna shook her head and hissed sympathetically as the goat fled into the huddle of animals, lurching on three legs. Instinct took it to seek shelter with its kind, but it carried its doom with it in the white bones poking through the skin, in the bloodstained hide, in the useless hoof hanging by a scrap of skin, and the nervous shuffling of the other goats showed their awareness of it.

"No more to do," said Anna, and we left.

And there is the head in the meat department. I have no way of knowing if it belonged to a goat; if I ask and someone understands, they'll probably say it's a sheep. Even if it is a goat, there is no guarantee it's the *same* goat; it could just be coincidence. But this is a place where things go on sale when they're available: fish, when the fishermen actually catch something; tomatoes, when there are too many ripening to eat all at once; newspapers, when the bus from Kalamata arrives. It isn't too far-fetched to think of a goatherd making a virtue of necessity when a goat kept for milking is injured beyond redemption.

But it brings animal husbandry into sharp focus. For once, the food on sale in a store has a face, so to speak. The whole business of human beings raising animals for their own benefit, feeding them and fattening them up just to kill and eat them, is abominable once the animals are personalized. Worse, by far, is that most of us are far too squeamish to do it for ourselves. Instead, we relish our steaks at a safe remove, further insulated by plastic wrap and styrofoam packaging from the reek of urine and dung, the stun guns and knives in the abattoirs, and the animals bawling in fear at the smell of blood and death as they wait their turn for execution.

That head brings the dark side of the meat industry all too close for comfort. It sits there as a raw, brutal memento mori, a reminder not only of man's predatory nature but also of the chanciness of existence—just a moment's inattention, a small clumsiness, a lapse of judgment, and life has gone.

ON CATS

Although unbearably itchy rashes tended to erupt around my chin and neck at the most fleeting contact with any feline when I was a child, I have enjoyed the company of many cats in my life.

The first, when I was about thirteen, was Timmy, a farmyard kitten rescued from certain drowning when I was on holiday in Somerset with my best friend, staying with her grandparents. He was not yet weaned, and we found ourselves in the heavy darkness of a sleeping cottage, heating milk in a teaspoon over a candle flame for a desperately mewling infant. He survived my parents' shock at his arrival, and a cold that gummed his eyes and dribbled from his nose and made his tiny chest heave and wheeze with every breath. He grew into an aloof tabby with a muscular tail and tufts on his ears that always suggested the feral creature beneath the glossy stripes.

In Merritt, our first home after immigrating to Canada in 1967, we had three cats who used to assemble in a semicircle round my son's high chair at every meal and wait for the manna to rain from heaven. My son was prone to tipping his dish upside down on top of his head and the cats learned quickly. The two females also produced litters of kittens in cupboards, astonishingly varied in colour as if they were flaunting their promiscuity.

When we moved to Pender Harbour we took the survivor of this trio with us, a beautiful plush blue-grey tomcat with eyes like peeled green grapes, who crept quietly into a garden shed one day to die. There we also had Wilson, a ginger tom, found abandoned in a ditch, who disappeared without trace. Then Sheba, a gorgeous, long-haired lilac point Siamese, who became the victim of her own fearless rat-hunting skills when she was run over by a car on her way to the ornamental pheasant cages across the road.

Later, in Fort St. James, there was the majestic Felix who left home for a three-month holiday every summer, returning promptly every year on August 28 after filling the neighbourhood with little barley-coloured clones. At the same time we lived with Beaker, white and elegantly thin, so called because he sounded like the hapless character on *The Muppets*, who dwindled in a week from feline leukemia. And there was Orlando, who appeared at the window one day and stayed for ten years, and Pushti, the tiny Siamese who welcomed us to her house when we moved and let us look after her until she died in her twenty-second year.

They are all there, cozy in memory, intact and self-sufficient and purring. But there is one with a more visceral hold, one I never owned, whom I knew for mere weeks but could never forget. Her only name was Cat.

We were staying at Koroni Camping, not in a tent, as it happened, but in a small house on the campground, surrounded by olive trees. The rather odd-looking Siamese belonging to Anna, the campsite owner, regularly wandered into the house looking for handouts, but there was also a small army of cats about the place, scrawny and unlovely for the most part. In the way of feral animals they slunk about, belly to the ground, scuttling across exposed areas to the shelter of trees and shrubs. Their ears were ragged, their faces scarred and scabbed, their fur dusty and brittle-looking.

Cat was one of those half-wild creatures, but she was young, not yet battered by living rough. She sauntered onto the veranda one day, investigated thoroughly, hopped up onto a chair and started washing herself. Her assurance immediately set her apart. She looked healthy and relatively clean; her black and white fur shone. She was hungry, though, and for good reason; her goat-shaped body revealed that she was pregnant. She wolfed down two plates of bread and milk and looked for more. We invested in a bag of cat biscuits.

In that way cats have of simultaneously serving their own interests and making you feel privileged, she adopted us. She would appear for meals and stay to sit on my lap or beside me as I read in the shade. She purred as I stroked her head or removed the ticks that swelled like blueberries near her eyes. To all intents and purposes, she became the family cat. We worried vaguely about what her fate would be after we left.

One afternoon I found her on my bed. I was chiefly concerned about the possibility of sleeping with vermin, and shooed her away, back outside. With the benefit of hindsight, I'm sure she was making a nest for her kittens, and I wish I'd had the gumption to find a box for her so that she could have stayed on the veranda or even in the house. She had her babies that night in the back storage area of the empty café on the site.

Anna told us about them. Cat had produced five kittens, all black and white like her. We saw little of her for a day or two, and we deduced that she was happily occupied with her family, but all was not well. Cat was disturbed about something; she moved her kittens from the café one by one and hid them under the shrubs growing by the wall along the road.

It was soon obvious what had induced her to give up the relative safety of the building: another cat had appeared, a large ginger tom, hunger on four legs, prowling as relentless and cold as a shark. Cat became an Amazon. We heard howls and bloodcurdling screeches in the bushes; saw Cat make desperate rushes from her hiding place, snarling and hissing; saw her launch herself at the ginger cat's haunches and transform them both into a whirling, yowling tangle of teeth and claws and flying limbs. For the very first time, I found myself looking for stones to throw at an animal, anything to help Cat demolish the enemy.

But it wasn't enough. Inexorably, the kittens disappeared one by one. I was out by the pool and heard yet another fight, saw the ginger cat streaking away. Cat appeared. She walked toward me, carrying something in her mouth. When she reached me, she dropped the bundle by my foot, looked at me and miaowed. She nudged the kitten with her nose, as if prompting it to get up, and mewed again. I picked the kitten up. It was completely limp, boneless, untouched apart from a slight dampness on the fur round its neck and a fleck of blood by its ear, warm as fresh toast.

Cat twined about my legs, looking up. I knew she expected me to help. I crouched down beside her, stroking the kitten lying on the palm of my hand and encouraging her to sniff at it. Hadn't I read somewhere that animals can smell death? Wouldn't Cat recognize what had happened and abandon the kitten?

Apparently not. I found myself trying to explain matters to her, apologizing for my own uselessness, but she persisted, nudging at the kitten and mewing. I had no means of hacking a grave for it in the rock-hard red soil; there was no convenient garbage bin. Finally I distracted Cat with food and quickly sought out a place to lay the tiny corpse and cover it with dead leaves.

Cat wandered off abstractedly. She stayed away for the next couple of days, and I thought of her alone, grieving for her kittens, teats swollen and sore.

The next afternoon she silently crept into the house, jumped onto a chair and dropped what she was carrying.

"Oh Cat, no!"

Pity forced out the words. Cat crouched over her dead kitten. The dust on its fur had faded the black to a dull brown and the body had the flattened look of old shoes. I was mesmerized by the image of Cat roaming the campsite, searching and searching for her dead baby, the maternal instinct reaching beyond the grave, when she crouched lower, took the kitten's head in her jaws and bit down.

For a second I couldn't take in what she was doing. The next instant, despite the voice which was stuttering rationalizations in my ear—it's instinctive, she's removing all traces that make her vulnerable, she needs the protein—revulsion took over and I wrestled the remains from her, rushed outside and flung them away over the wall, out of sight, as far away as possible, just so that I didn't have to see her cannibalize her young, do the unthinkable, taint her sweet domestic image.

We did not see much of her after that, just fleeting appearances of a black-and- white wraith slipping in and out of the shadows. Her brief flirtation with humans had brought her little besides disillusionment, and she had returned to her nomadic existence. If she lived very long, she no doubt lost her glossy vitality, leached away by repeated pregnancies and chronic malnourishment. She probably became part of the ginger tomcat's harem, still dominated by the murderer of her firstborn. No doubt she had scars and torn ears, bald patches and harsh fur.

But she would also have been as canny as an animal can ever be, sly and cunning and resourceful in ways I can never match. Courageous I know she was; stoic, too, beyond endurance. An altogether admirable animal. My superior intelligence was of no use within the raw parameters of her world; we have come too far from our animal roots to be able to cope with nature red in tooth and claw.

It is unlikely that we will ever have to, perhaps. But Cat is a reminder of a reality that our urbanized life has almost concealed—the constant danger of the wild animal's existence, a passionless ferocity for which we are entirely unequipped—which lies in wait for us if we are ever stupid enough to bring about the destruction of civilization.

ARCTOPHILIA

He lives on in my daughter's house, sustained by sentiment, for he is neither use nor ornament. Once upon a time, when my aunt first gave him to me after scouring the empty toyshop shelves in late 1940, he had long gold fur and warm amber eyes. I remember the velvet softness of his paws, the solidity of his body, the invisible button in the middle of his stomach that produced a deep lowing moo when pressed. Teddy is the only tangible survivor of my infancy.

By the time my own daughter unaccountably adopted him as her own in 1971, he was a shadow of his former self. He was largely bald, with patches of grubby fur on limbs and ears like a victim of a serious case of mange. Both eyes had disappeared. He had lost a considerable amount of his stuffing, which seemed to be a mixture of sawdust and hay, and his limbs dangled as if the muscles had atrophied, while his face had collapsed about the nose. The metal button in his stomach now protruded, but was silent.

At the time, we were living for a while with my mother-in-law in England. Together, my three-year-old daughter and her grandmother set about Teddy's rehabilitation. The obvious leaks were sewn up.

Teddy acquired new eyes—large, round, white cloth-covered buttons which reminded me of Little Orphan Annie, and, far from restoring his sight, seemed to emphasize his blindness. For the very first time, he acquired clothes, and in the process, underwent a sex change; he now wore a knitted green skirt with shoulder straps. For reasons unknown, and unknowable except to a toddler, my daughter renamed him Brussel (after Brussels sprouts) and made him her constant companion. And now, nearly seventy years old, my contemporary moulders on, revered but set aside, thousands of miles from his birthplace, the decaying victim of too much love.

There is nothing unique about this story. Versions of it must abound, for surely most children in the western hemisphere count a teddy bear among their favourite stuffed toys, and have done for more than a hundred years. And the affection survives childhood; it is, after all, adults who buy babies their first toys, and they tend to purchase their own lingering memories of comforting softness and warmth, of constancy, of a size that matched their own, of companionship, of a benign gaze that never altered. Adults justify the existence of those stores with cute names that sell nothing but teddies of every size, shape and colour, clothed and unclothed; adults crowd auctions and flea markets in the hope of acquiring antique teddy aristocrats.

Other adults gave us Winnie the Pooh—the quintessential teddy, a good listener, kind, patient, faithful, always optimistic and tolerant of others, ready to follow and not overwhelmingly bright, a sort of Dr. Watson for the nursery set—closely followed by Rupert and Paddington Bear, and a whole bevy of lesser literary, cartoon, and television bears, solo and *en famille*. These are just some of the bears that are characters in their own right, but the appetite for them does not stop there. Even fictional characters, not necessarily human, have their teddies: Lord Sebastian Flyte in *Brideshead Revisited* had Aloysius; Mr. Bean constantly talked to his battered teddy; Radar in *M*A*S*H** had an anonymous bear, and in a graceful homage, Big Bird had Radar; even the dreadful cat Garfield has Pooky. Inevitably, teddies have infiltrated video games as well, perversely becoming villains in the guise of the Nazi-style Tediz in Nintendo's *Conker* series. Which all leads to a question: why has this particular animal gained such an iconic status?

Going back to the origin of the teddy bear is not much help. There are several versions of the story: servants at the hunting lodge console Teddy Roosevelt for a trophy-less day with the small stuffed bears they have made; the president orders the humane dispatch of a wounded bear that has killed some of the dogs, thus demonstrating his concern for wildlife; after a disappointing day's hunting, Roosevelt refuses to kill a small bear his guides manage to capture, thus showing his sportsmanlike qualities and compassion, and inspiring a celebrated political cartoon. Whichever version approximates the truth of the incident, the popularity of the ensuing stuffed toys obviously owes nothing to the celebrity of Teddy Roosevelt: nobody gives that somewhat eccentric president a second thought nowadays. If they had been merely an offshoot of the Roosevelt culture, teddy bears would have been as ephemeral an enthusiasm as Tickle Me Elmo or Cabbage Patch dolls.

The teddy mythology does highlight one significant point: the stuffed toys may be the embodiment of cute and cuddly, but the original models are large wild animals, clever and dangerous. There is a huge disparity between the real thing and the toy, and one which most people never get to measure at first hand.

Europeans, like me, tend to have little experience of bears in the wild. For one thing, there is not much wild left, especially in Western Europe, and the indigenous bear has declined even in those parts which still offer it some living space. Certainly, apart from a pathetic creature I once saw, tethered by a chain at the edge of a gypsy encampment in former Yugoslavia, no doubt condemned to dance for pennies, I had never seen a bear of any kind outside a zoo until I came to North America.

A camping trip into the Rockies not long after our arrival in Canada changed that. Suddenly, bears were everywhere. For us, they made an entirely original traffic hazard, plodding calmly across the highway, indifferent to our approach. Ponderous black forms lumbered out of ditches and down slopes with that peculiar rolling gait that seems to rotate their rear ends. We saw them eating berries, wading in streams, sitting half-concealed by vegetation while their cubs played at their side.

The road was lined with notices warning the public not to feed the bears. The public, naturally, ignored them, swerving onto the shoulders of the road wherever they saw bears waiting, or wherever some other traveller had already lured the animals to his vehicle. We lost count of the number of times we saw cars parked right beside the warning signs, hands tossing stale sandwiches and the like to the waiting mouths, while other hands frantically manipulated cameras to record the encounters.

One image has always stayed with me from that journey. Two bears, an adult and a large cub, standing on their hind legs alongside a station wagon, front paws braced against the car's body, heads inside, as if they were neighbours leaning in at the open windows to chat. I have often wondered what the occupants would have done if the bears had tried to join them, whether they still have all their fingers and hands, whether the owner found any gouges in his paintwork later, and felt a clammy frisson as he remembered the size of the claws curved over the bottom of the window frame, inches from his wife's head.

We had our own adventure on that trip, just as much the result of ignorance and naïveté.

The campground was not crowded and we easily found a secluded site for our tent trailer, near washrooms and firewood, but surrounded by dark trees. A large picnic table sat in the middle of the clearing. We had been intrigued by the campground's big garbage cans, hanging off the ground, with special lids that were complicated to remove. They suggested, far more urgently than the ubiquitous signs ever could, that bears were present and problematic. We took them seriously and carefully concealed our foodstuff away from the trailer, but looking back at our precautions, I am sure that we adopted them in a spirit of safeguarding the food supplies rather than our lives.

Obviously, the food sometimes has to come out of hiding. Early one morning, my husband had fired up the propane stove at the end of the picnic table and was preparing some quick oatmeal for breakfast. He had got as far as setting out some plates and cups, a packet of butter and some bread when he went to fill the kettle, taking our oldest son with him. I had just finished dressing our daughter, who was still a toddler. She climbed down from the trailer and clambered onto the seat of the picnic table, ready for breakfast. I turned my attention to our other son's attempts to get his shoes on.

My daughter's cry stilled my hands in mid-knot. She was standing on the bench, watching an adult black bear sniffing around the stove where the pot of porridge steamed. Even as I registered this, the bear, put off, perhaps, by the heat, abandoned that intriguing smell and investigated another. Facing my daughter across the table, front paws on the opposite bench, the bear snuffled around the tabletop and located the butter. Ignoring my daughter's crows of delight as she danced up and down, the bear gravely peeled back the foil wrapping and started to eat. The long pink tongue wrapped itself round the prize, then the teeth got to work, slicing off chunks. A pound of butter disappeared in far less time than it has taken to tell this story, and I was still rooted in the doorway of the trailer, trying to decide if it would be better to run and grab my daughter, or stay where I was and let the bear move away when there was nothing left to scavenge from the table.

At that moment, my husband and son returned. The bear did not hesitate. It snatched at the packet of bread as it dropped to all fours and lumbered away. My daughter cried in disappointment.

"If you go out in the woods today, you're sure of a big surprise . . ." We did and we were, but although I can recall the little clutch of fear that was the proper response to the unexpected presence of a powerful wild animal at the breakfast table, and a slightly panicked dithering about the most sensible course of action, I do not remember feeling that my daughter had been in any real danger. There was more the feeling that the bears had turned the tables on Goldilocks, amusement at the brazenness of the theft, a little open-mouthed marvelling that such creatures dwelt among us. "The Teddy Bear's Picnic" still obscured the real animal.

That changed, as everything does, with experience. Living in Fort St. James, a small town in north-central British Columbia, I found black bears a commonplace. Familiarity, they say, breeds contempt. Whoever coined that expression had never lived in a place that a bear considered part of his own range, never logged or planted trees in bear territory alone and far from any help. He had never climbed a tree to get away from a bear, desperately kicking at the animal's head as it clawed at his feet, nor been frozen in shock at the realization that he stood between a bear and her cub. He had not hurried away from a patch of wild raspberries at the sound of a heavy body approaching through the bush, as yet invisible, but careless, bending and snapping branches, making no secret of its presence and intent on eating the very same berries. He had never cowered in his house, listening to the claws ripping the mesh in the screen doors, or woken in a tent to find a bear trying to tear its way in.

All these things happened, though not to me, personally. They were part of bear knowledge, the kind of folklore that arms those who can encounter bears at any time. In the North, black bears were our neighbours, especially when we lived outside the town itself. Unless they were injured or starving, they kept to themselves, but they were a constant presence. While I was gardening, I would hear them plodding through the bush, unmistakably weighty and bulky. They would roam about the orchard, helping themselves to apples, sitting on their haunches under the trees and reaching up to pull down a more inaccessible branch. I have seen trees split in half by bears, fresh white wounds from mutilated branches bleeding sap, the slow, patient growing nullified by impatience and awesome strength. On walks, I have come across saucer-shaped depressions in long grass where bears have slept, and piles of bear scat loaded with purple Saskatoon berries. I have shooed a bear away from my apple trees by flinging my arms over my head to make myself look big, jumping up and down and shouting, only to watch it retreat behind the barn, and then peep at me round the corner of the building.

Once, walking along a forest trail with the dog, I met a bear coming round a curve in the opposite direction. Both of us stopped dead, while the dog, clueless, pottered on, sniffing the ground between us. There was a nasty moment while I anticipated the dog walking into trouble, running past me to hide, and leading the bear straight to me, and the bear seemed to be weighing its options, too, but then it turned aside and crashed into the undergrowth. I could hear its retreat down the hill and breathed a sigh of relief; the dog simply looked enquiringly into the bushes as the snaps and rustles faded away. Thereafter, I adopted the habit of jingling coins or wearing bear bells in the woods.

Sometimes, we could frighten the bears, but they had to be young. On one occasion I heard the familiar sounds coming through the woods behind our house—familiar, but magnified, as if a small army were slogging through the trees. Three cubs, teenagers, wandered one by one into view. They stopped when I stood up on my deck to see them better, and with one accord, scrambled up three separate trees, and clung there high off the ground, watching my every move until I took pity on them and went inside.

Setting cameos like this aside—they are hardly typical—nobody who is accustomed to bears sees them as cute and cuddly. Instead, the bear has *gravitas*, a dignity that magnetically accumulates myth and legend. Effortlessly, they embody qualities that we find familiar or could admire in ourselves: intelligence, self-sufficiency, omnivorous appetites, controlled power, the stern loneliness that sets them wandering their vast territories in a single-minded drive for survival. So much of their lives is mysterious. We have got beyond the early bestiarists' bemused observation that bears eat ants when sick and produce shapeless lumps when they give birth— "very tiny pulps of a white colour, with no eyes"—which they then lick into shape, but we still have to acknowledge that, like Howard Hughes, they are secretive recluses, and like him, never completely knowable: elusive forms in the shadows of the forests. And what other large mammal can sleep through the cold of winter, suspending life to a whisper, and not only survive to emerge, but lead a new generation into another spring? Resurrection has always been the magic trick of the gods.

All the more tragic, then, that bears rarely emerge well from encounters with humans. We usurp their range, strew our prodigal waste across their landscape, and bisect their migration routes with roaring highways. Then, when they investigate the landfills and become addicted to the easy pickings of garbage, when hunger in lean years drives them into our gardens, when they cause accidents by following ancestral paths across four lanes of asphalt, they are labelled nuisance bears, and one way or another, removed.

One of the saddest stories I ever heard about so-called nuisance bears was related to me by a young colleague. While still a student, he had been staying with his grandmother, sleeping in her basement. One morning, he awoke late, alone in the house. A bleary glance through the window alerted him to the presence of a black bear in the back yard. It was eating apples, and helping itself to berries. It was a beautiful day, he said, and the bear's innocent enjoyment of the food, its leisurely, contented ambling about the garden was so endearing that he stayed at the window watching, sharing an idyllic moment as if they were the only two living creatures in the world. Then, the bear jerked, keeled over, and lay still.

For a moment, the young man could not believe his eyes, waited for the bear to get up, shake itself and move away. When it didn't, he raced outside—and discovered RCMP officers with rifles in the garden and a good crowd of neighbours in front of the house.

"Apparently there'd been lots of complaints about the bear," he said, "but I didn't know. I'd never seen it before."

He glanced away, and fiddled with his glass of beer, obviously reliving the waste and betrayal of that far-off morning in the sun.

"It wasn't doing any harm," he said.

That story brings home the ambivalence we feel about bears. On the one hand, we sentimentalize them, make cuddlesome toys and storybook characters with very human qualities out of them. At the opposite extreme, as happened with the so-called spirit bears of the Pacific coast, we invest them with almost religious significance in our admiration for their strength and grandeur, and our guilt at endangering them, weaving them into myth and legend as the guardians of the land. Nevertheless, mankind continues to gobble up their habitat, or indirectly ruin it, threatening their very survival: many kinds of Asian bears are extinct;

hardly any bears remain in the Pyrenees, in Italy or in Greece; the polar bear is in serious trouble because the sea ice is melting and cutting it off from its food source. If bears wander into our neighbourhoods, we shoot them or haul them miles away; poachers kill them to feed the dreadful appetite for bear gall bladders in traditional Chinese medicine; they used to be reluctant participants in spectator sports like bear baiting, and, while performing bears are no longer in fashion, the last time I saw it, the Moscow Circus still had bears riding bicycles as one of its acts.

We love them, but we don't hesitate to exploit and victimize them; we admire, even revere them, but at the same time we fear them. And with good reason. I am writing this in the very week that two serious grizzly attacks in the Rockies hit the headlines. Teddy Bear has his dark side. And oddly enough, it's all there in that relentlessly jolly song about the picnic, in one of the verses that nobody remembers:

> If you go out in the woods today,
> You'd better not go alone.
> It's lovely out in the woods today,
> But safer to stay at home.

Puts an entirely different light on my battered old Brussel.

LOVING A WALL

Once upon a time, I lived in the Central Interior of British Columbia, about one hundred and ten miles northwest of Prince George as the crow flies, in the town of Fort St. James. There I became a landowner, as opposed to a mere homeowner with the usual garden patch, edges firmly defined by chain-link or privet. When I moved to my house on its nearly eight acres of largely uncleared bush, there was no wall or fence between me and my neighbour on his treeless five-acre lot. There seemed no need. Nothing was more in keeping with the rural character of the place than the unobstructed boundary between the properties.

But that was before I experienced my neighbour's hobbies.

Axel was what is euphemistically called a diamond in the rough. He worked in the mill; he had a pit bull named Barney permanently attached to a ramshackle dog house; he hurled horseshoes in his front yard, beer in hand, cursing the blackflies; he was never happier than when he was hurtling about on a skidoo or encased in black leather on his motor bike with his wife, Eva, wedged behind him.

He was kindly, too; when I got myself stuck helplessly in the partially melted snowbanks on my driveway, it was Axel who roared up in his pick-up, lassoed a tree and winched me out.

I always knew when spring was truly established: some people have swallows returning; I had the first sighting of Axel shirtless, his pallid torso offered to the feeble sun. With the spring plumage came seasonal cries; my neighbour's vocabulary was repetitive and highly audible.

This was entertaining in a way, and all would have been well, except that Axel turned to husbandry.

Year One. Axel chose pigs. The animals were kept, not twenty feet from his back door, in a makeshift pen flung together from the odd-ments of wood and corrugated metal scattered over the property. They were never actually visible, apart from brief glimpses of muddy backs or snouts, until the morning I wandered blearily into the kitchen, gazed out of the window and saw that a Heath Robinson gallows, rather like the devices people erect over their cars to pull out the engine, had material-ized in Axel's yard. Wreathed in steam from a vat of boiling water, my neighbour was straining to haul a long pink carcass into the air. The pig's ears flapped pathetically over its nose at each jerk. Axel was about to scrape the bristles off its skin. I must have come late to the spectacle, but it snatched me back to an afternoon of my tenth year when I lis-tened, appalled, to the terrified shrieks of a pig being slaughtered coming from the barn at the end of my cousin's garden. At least I had missed the demise of Axel's animals. Ever after, the pigpen remained in the yard, unoccupied.

Year Two. Axel obviously decided that pigs were too labour-intensive so he opted for an animal that would more or less look after itself, given all the grass that surrounded his house. One day I had to rub my eyes in disbelief. There was a white rabbit by the side of Axel's house. And another. And another. And another. I felt like Alice in Wonderland.

I never found out how many rabbits there were. At least twenty. The amazing thing was that they stayed where they were, giving the pit bull a wide berth. Apparently they hopped into one of the decrepit sheds at night. But there came a day when they all disappeared simultaneously. I assumed that Axel had got through the pork chops and his freezer was full again.

I say they all disappeared, but there were two fugitives. Terror sent them hopping headlong into strange territory. They crossed the unmarked boundary and took up residence under my deck. I purchased rabbit pellets, which they accepted with every indication of enthusiasm. But they were doomed. Their screams in the night when they both fell victim to a fox were horrifying. Axel's hobbies were taking a serious toll on my equanimity.

Year Three. Axel made the wrong choice. Perhaps he was aiming at something unique. Maybe he aspired to the aesthetic rather than the purely utilitarian. That year he proudly released two large birds into the back yard. Obviously he was expecting them to be homebodies, like the rabbits.

They were rounded, pear shaped, like very large quail. They had astonishing voices. They ran widdershins about the house, screaming. Then the two guinea fowl paused, consulted and lifted off together to disappear into the poplars across the road. Axel's son was sent off in pursuit. As he crashed noisily in the undergrowth, two dark shapes broke from the tree tops and headed silently north. The youth returned empty-handed.

"Fuck the fucking birds," said Axel.

To compensate, Axel went in for geese. They were elegant birds and sociable. They quickly decided the grass was greener on the other side of the non-existent fence, and visited us frequently. They were partial to the tender shoots of young vegetables, but I become fond of them, especially when they produced goslings. I watched them grow up, chased them away from my annuals and provided them with large buckets of water from which they drank together, long white necks dipping and rising like pump handles.

The Day of Reckoning came for them, too. Once again, two escaped. The parents made off, waddling across my yard, through the orchard, into the trees and down to the creek. There they stayed, sculling about on the water, causing passing motorists to do double takes.

But winter was their enemy.

Inexorably, the water in the creek froze, shrinking their swimming area until a mere puddle remained. That froze over, too. Then they huddled miserably on the ice. I threw grain onto the ice from the bridge, and they came for it in an ungainly scramble, necks outstretched, webbed feet slithering. They were dreadfully vulnerable without the water.

One morning, there was just one left. It, too, was doomed. The next day, it had gone. I could hardly bear Axel's hobbies anymore.

Year Four. Axel had ambitions. I could see him, crashing about in a stand of saplings near the invisible fence line. Small trees fell to left and right to the whine of his chainsaw.

"Thinking of getting some cattle," he explained. "Just clearing for a fence."

Thinking about it must have been too exhausting. The steers never materialized. Nor did the fence. Instead, Axel let loose a rooster in charge of some fifteen or twenty hens. They were truly free-range birds. They quickly abandoned Axel's field and ranged freely over my garden. They appreciated newly tilled earth where I had just planted peas. I replanted these three times before I caught on and tried to construct a barrier round the vegetable garden. They took nips out of leaves, scratched up seedlings, had ecstatic dust baths in the planters.

In retaliation, I flew at them, shrieking and flailing brooms. I left my deadliest weapon, the garden hose, permanently uncoiled at the ready, and drove them back over the boundary like a riot policeman clearing a street with a water cannon. I aimed particularly for the rooster, the brains of the operation. There was a huge satisfaction in drenching him. I laughed as he shook himself just across the boundary after yet another rout. Water flying off his bedraggled feathers, he let out a bloodcurdling screech of frustration. I actually looked forward to the day when Axel would wring his neck.

But I was the one who caved in. The day after the hens scratched up all my infant carrots, I got fence posts hammered in. A friend rounded up two semi-willing youths and put up the wire netting. The chickens were finally defeated.

"Something there is that doesn't love a wall."

Certainly, building the fence filled me with regret. I came to have a lot of fellow-feeling for the other person in that poem by Robert Frost, though. "Good fences make good neighbours," he insists, doggedly replacing the fallen stones.

As my experiences proved, it is entirely possible to be of two minds. Land without any visible barriers echoes a state of nature, an ideal condition in which the human imprint is no more obtrusive than that of any other creature. Axel's animals were not at fault, but his fecklessness brought home how seriously one man's actions can affect others, and in that particular case, make me love a wall. Maybe we always carry the ambivalence about with us, leaning sometimes to the one side, sometimes the other, for both stances have their merits. I know I had both the characters of the poem facing each other over some crumbling wall in my own head. The hens tipped the balance in my case. Suddenly I understood the French, whose idea of the perfect garden always involves a high wall and a single gateway, with a locked door and a little bell for the visitor to ring.

Besides, I had a hunch about Year Five and needed a pre-emptive strike. Goats were on the cards.

THE UNREADY

I watch birds. Like most people, I put up a hummingbird feeder outside the window to observe the antics of those amazing little creatures in close-up. Near the middle of August one year, I became aware of an anomaly. For the very first time I saw a hummingbird who could only be described as a complete incompetent.

She was one of the wave of babies mobbing the feeder. (I say "she" as if I could actually identify the sex, but this is unscientific; I confess to using the feminine pronoun for no better reason than a strong feeling that it was accurate. Since I am not a scientist, I am unrepentant.) Like all the others, she was new to the game and hungry. But where her peers were small, she was minute; where their feathers already showed an iridescent green, she was still a downy grey ball; where they were a little slow and tentative, she was totally clueless.

Her behaviour was so bizarre that it made her an instant victim. I first noticed her, in fact, as the cowering target of multiple dive-bombing raids. Bickering is an automatic reflex for hummingbirds, whose aggression seems to be in inverse proportion to their size, but this was different. Against this apparently inoffensive fledgling, the attacks were calculated and remorseless. She was effectively being denied food.

She kept trying. The other babies had obviously figured out the mechanics of the feeder. They were busily dipping their beaks into the holes at the centre of the little yellow plastic flowers as if they had been programmed for it. Most of them had also realized that they didn't need to hover in front of their chosen spigot and could actually park on the tiny rail that encircled the feeder, thereby saving energy.

She didn't know any of this. Obviously she understood that the feeder represented food, but how to obtain it was a complete mystery. She had no idea where to stick her beak, which was about half regulation size, anyway. She kept stabbing at the petals of the plastic flowers, prying underneath them, poking the glass, hovering over the top of the feeder and hopelessly investigating the hole where the string comes through the cap.

Her fumbling infuriated the others. She was much too small to stand on the perch and reach the nectar, so she tried to stand on the body of the feeder and slithered about, her wings beating frantically. Failing to get any satisfaction from her own plastic flower, she would join a successfully slurping sibling at the next one, sitting on its head in her desperation to reach some food, trying to ram her beak in the same hole. Of course, she was driven off, again and again.

Her clumsy efforts made us christen her Bumblebeak. We became quite anxious about her, knowing how much hummingbirds must eat to survive. My mother, visiting from England and quite enchanted by the birds, became fiercely partisan.

"Leave him alone, you little beast!" she would command as yet another came in for the attack, beak open and claws out. (My mother, incidentally, was quite impervious to my perception that Bumblebeak was female. I think she felt it was impossible that a female could be so maladroit.)

By this time, Bumblebeak looked a bit the worse for wear. When perched, she hunched up in a ball; the feathers on the top of her head were ruffled and sticking up at odd angles. At every attack she would crouch down further and obviously hope for the best.

She turned her attention to real flowers next. Every hummingbird worth its salt ignores petunias, and smelling the way they do, you can't fault their judgment. Bumblebeak explored them exhaustively, disappearing entirely inside their bells. Then she found the delphiniums. At last! A flower that offered some nourishment!

But she quickly revealed that she was as clueless about real flowers as she was about plastic ones. If she got any nectar at all, it would have been by accident, for once again she stabbed furiously at every part of the flower but the right one. It was as if she had a dim notion of the principle, but had missed out completely on its practical applications.

I watched her clambering awkwardly over the delphinium spikes and shook my head. It seemed more and more unlikely that she could survive on her own. My feeling was reinforced when I saw her later that evening, sitting on the deck, forced down by aerial bombardment and exhaustion. The last sighting I had that day was of her clinging grimly to the siding of the house like a pygmy woodpecker, having been thwarted once again in her attempt to reach the feeder.

We didn't see her at all the next day and it seemed as if our worst fears had been realized.

But on the third day, there she was again. Miraculously, she had sorted out how to eat. She still couldn't reach the feeder when perched, but she was finally getting her beak into the right place. The others still attacked, but she would stand her ground and open her beak defiantly, and their attacks grew more mechanical and absent-minded. She even seemed a little larger and her feathers were no longer ruffled.

She would survive, at least for the immediate future.

"Poor little thing," said my mother, "what a start to life. His mother must have gone away without teaching him how to do anything."

While it is probably true that Bumblebeak's parents had taken off for greener pastures with the cheerful ruthlessness of adults conscious of a gruelling job well done, leaving their offspring to hone their skills before embarking on the journey to Mexico, it is unfair to regard them as derelict in their duties. The miracle with most animals, not just hummingbirds, is how few Bumblebeaks there are.

In the natural world there is a huge stylistic range in the rearing of young, from complete non-participation, as in cuckoos laying their eggs in the nests of other, more responsible birds, or frogs leaving their spawn attached to the underside of lily pads, to the many years of active involvement by large mammals such as elephants and whales, the great apes and humans. In general, long-lived, intellectually well-endowed species spend a lot more time ushering their young from complete dependence to self-sufficiency. They simply have more to learn.

At least, that's what we humans tell ourselves. Yet, when you come right down to it, all living creatures, including humans, are concerned with only three basic things: having enough to eat, finding adequate shelter, and reproducing their own kind. The imperatives are identical for a dragonfly and a Komodo dragon; how admirable, then, that so many creatures can equip their young to meet these needs independently in a very short time.

Merely a few short days take a naked hummingbird chick, newly hatched from its pea-sized egg, to fully fledged aggression at the feeder. It knows which parts of which flowers will supply nectar, it can hover and fly backwards, defend itself and find shelter in woodpiles at night. With such a skill-set to pass on, and such a limited time in which to do it, small wonder that the parents cannot lavish attention on the chick that hatches two days later than the others, always gets pushed to the bottom of the nest when food appears, and isn't quite ready to fly when its siblings first try their wings. The Bumblebeaks sink or swim; presumably, the clutches are large enough to compensate for unavoidable attrition. If the chick survives the parents' defection, it can set off, without ever having done it before, on a journey of thousands of miles and arrive at exactly the same place its forebears have frequented for generations. Then, when the time is right, it turns around and comes back to the place where it first saw the light. If it is a male, it knows how to stake out a territory and perform dazzling aerial displays, climbing to stalling point and diving and climbing again, to impress a nearby female sitting quietly in a bush. And the birds know how to weave a perfect nest like a tiny grass hammock lined with moss and down to swing from a twig, and how to rear the occupants of the Lilliputian eggs.

Ah, we say, but that's just instinct. That's not like learning the times tables or playing the piano or becoming a grand master in chess. Certainly no other animal will write a *War and Peace*, or paint a Sistine Chapel, or split an atom, and we may be rightly proud of human achievement and the way mankind never stops demanding more and more of the brain, but that does not justify the slightly smug self-congratulation of that "just." Instinct is different from learned knowledge, not inferior.

In fact, the abilities conferred by instinct seem nothing short of miraculous to humans who do not share them. There are so many marvels: migrations of birds, of whales, of fish, of land animals like the caribou, of insects like the Monarch butterfly, undertaken without any maps or instructions, any perceptible signposts or vehicles or helpful travel agents; the amazing endurance of the Emperor penguins, trudging to and fro between the sea and the nesting area inland, starving for months as they incubate the eggs in the middle of the Antarctic winter; the inborn guidance system that makes newly hatched turtles dig themselves out of the sand and sends them scrambling for the unknown sea where they will spend the rest of their lives; the exquisite sensitivity that determines the exact amount of rotting vegetation an alligator mother piles on her clutch of eggs to produce the optimum temperature for successful hatching.

How do they do it? we wonder. How do they know? We can theorize about successful adaptation, survival of the fittest and genetic information. Observation and research may reveal special organs—like the heat-detecting equipment in the snake's tongue, for example, that compensates for its poor eyesight—that may account for an animal's ability. We watch migrations and speculate about the possible use of magnetic fields, or navigation by stars or sun and moon, or recognition of the smells of earth or vegetation or water. We can come up with all sorts of plausible ideas; to repair our own deficiencies, we can even invent global positioning devices that will tell us the way to any address anywhere in the world. The fact remains, though, that if *we* left home as babies, never informed of its whereabouts, spent our lives thousands of miles away and then felt compelled to return, we would never find our birthplaces unaided in a million years. Yet salmon do it all the time.

The really interesting question is not why animals have such deeply entrenched instincts. It is why we don't. We have certain impulses—loving our children, for example, and fearing snakes—that we dignify as instinctive, and they probably are, since they may contribute to the survival of ourselves or of our kind, but we play them down, call them "feelings," which instantly betrays our sense that they are not as reliable as rational thought. Yet while it has brought us many gifts, the brain has led us further and further away from our animal connection to the earth: we are more familiar with the smell of hydrocarbons than the smell of rain about to fall; the din that assails our ears is so constant that we find silence troubling; we do not know the stars because the light pollution from our cities hides them from us. No surprise, then, that we cannot feel the magnetic pull of the Earth, or read the currents of the air and sea, or chart our course by scent or temperature; we are much too clever for that.

But we admire those who can and do, even envy them a little. Animals move intuitively in their worlds, immune to doubt, focused entirely on the essentials of existence. Driven and protected by their instincts, always attuned to their surroundings, they are fully occupied with being themselves. And how good they are at it! Nothing can be as much of a dog as a dog; a hummingbird is quintessentially a hummingbird, never a parrot.

A highly evolved brain is a wonderful asset. No human should be without one. It's worth remembering though, that most of the inhabitants of this planet rely far more on their senses and their instincts than on cognitive ability. They may not rule the world—and interestingly, have never shown any indication that they would want to—but the rarity of an anomaly like Bumblebeak merely serves to underline how successful they are at life and living.

CROWS

One of my favourite childhood memories stars my usually prosaic father, prompted, perhaps, by the sight of black shapes perched in a tree or on a fence, reciting a verse of poetry with relish. It was the only time his voice betrayed his origins; in his version, remembered from an Edwardian boyhood, the ghost of his Norfolk accent made a single rhyme of all the end words:

> Two old crows sat on a gate;
> One old crow said to his mate
> "What shall we have this day to eat?"
> "I know, we'll have some of this farmer's wheat!"

Later on, when I became interested in the Border ballads, I recognized this as a diluted, domesticated form of a much older oral tradition. In "The Twa Corbies," for example, the answer to the question "Where sall we gang and dine to-day?" is an old (probably neglected) ditch where the body of a "new slain knight" lies hidden, the location known only to the man's hawk, hound, and "lady fair." The hawk and hound are off hunting, and the lady has "ta'en another mate," so the crows have no competition.

"Ye'll sit on his white hause-bane,
And I'll pike out his bonny blue een;
Wi ae lock o his gowden hair
We'll theek our nest when it grows bare.

"Mony a one for him makes mane,
But nane sall ken where he is gane;
Oer his white banes, when they are bare,
The wind sall blaw for evermair."

The cynical birds preside like black spirits over an elegiac tale of love betrayed and lonely death.

These two fragments of folk tradition embody many of the reasons for the hostility this family of birds often encounters. It is all there, too, in the collective nouns for the various species that make up the crow family: a mob of crows, a scold of jays, a clattering of choughs, a tiding of magpies, a murder or an unkindness of ravens. For the superstitious, their blackness immediately suggests the forces of darkness, and when that is allied to their appetite for carrion, the connection is reinforced. They are harbingers of death, drawn to dissolution, and have been the grim reapers at times of battle, slaughter, and plague since time immemorial: profiting, it seems, from suffering.

They are blamed for the disappearance of songbirds, because of their raids on eggs and nestlings. They are accused of ruining crops by stealing seeds that have just been planted. Bounties are placed on their heads; in some places people are encouraged to shoot crows, and many a farmer will hang the corpse of a crow beside a field as a deterrent if his scarecrows don't work. Every year someone complains about crows dive-bombing passersby; in the city where I live, politicians and civil servants have been denied their usual access to the legislature on occasion by angry birds attacking their heads.

The crow family as a whole suffers from bad press, but it is utterly undeserved. There is not much that can be done about superstition, but we should be glad that crows and their relatives enjoy eating dead things. Without the carrion eaters acting as volunteer garbage collectors, the inevitable decay of all organic material would be far more of a problem for us than it is. The birds are certainly predators and they *do* steal the eggs and nestlings of other birds, but if there is an attendant decline in the population of smaller birds, it is far more likely to be the result of pollution or loss of habitat—our fault, in other words—than of the crows' depredations. Like most animal predators, crows take only what they need. They do eat seed; they are, after all, omnivorous. But, as Candace Savage points out in her lovely book on the crow family, *Bird Brains*, their consumption of seed is petty theft at worst; one study she quotes concluded that only 1 per cent of the food eaten by crows during a seeding season in New York state was corn. By contrast, another study revealed that just one family of crows consumed about forty thousand agricultural insect pests in nesting time. Even the crows' habit of aerial bombardment has its benign aspect when we look at it from their point of view. Crows pair for life and make excellent parents; that nest the Twa Corbies planned to upholster with hair would be fiercely protected. The RCMPs and deputy ministers forced to run or protect themselves with umbrellas were simply trespassers, walking too close to the nestlings.

The truth is that crows and their many cousins are fascinating birds. Like us, they are everywhere: the only places on Earth that do not have resident representatives of the family are the Antarctic and New Zealand. Again like us, they are distinguished by their intelligence; any human observer of the birds will have felt the little shock of delighted recognition at their cleverness and their ability to solve problems, the conspiratorial pleasure in their mischief and their sense of humour.

That humans have always recognized a sort of kindred spirit in these birds is obvious from the stories we have told ourselves for centuries. Aesop's thirsty crow, dropping pebbles into the jug to raise the level of the water, could obviously hold its own with Archimedes. On a more spiritual level, the crow family, specifically the raven, is the subject of a cycle of myths from the top of the world, stories told across Siberia and North America. In these, Raven is the creator of the world. Unlike his humourless Judeo-Christian counterpart, Raven enjoys practical jokes and fun. In a moment of boredom, he adds genitals to his creations, thus starting a novel new game. It is this jocular, sometimes malicious creature that Bill Reid depicts in his famous sculpture of the enormous raven coaxing the tiny humans, who are terrified of his shadow, from the shelter of their clam shell.

Ravens appear in significant roles in other northern cultures. In Norse myth, the god Odin has two ravens called Thought and Memory. They are a two-bird spy network: they circumnavigate the world every day and return at night to report everything they have seen. The Irish, too, have a special place for ravens; the expression "raven's knowledge" refers to the ability to know everything in the past and future.

The Romans relied heavily on augury to make their decisions, and their priests fulfilled their role in part by interpreting the croaking of ravens in order to foretell the future.

Even in the modern world, at least one tradition involving ravens lingers on. Legend has it that as long as ravens remain at the Tower of London, it cannot fall. So there have been resident ravens at the Tower for centuries, carefully looked after by their own attendants, protected in time of war, and now, insulated from any possible contact with avian flu from wild birds. Maybe it is coincidence, but the last successful invasion of England was William the Conqueror's—the very man who built the Tower of London.

Iconic status can only be born of accumulated knowledge. Ravens and their relatives profit by remaining close to human habitation; there has always been ample opportunity to observe these birds and learn their nature. Many people have crow stories, related for the most part with affection or amusement, or even awe. Personal contact always modifies the black-hearted harbinger of doom persona wished upon the crow family by superstition and perpetuated in the work of such disparate artists as Edgar Allan Poe and Alfred Hitchcock.

Close encounters of the corvid kind began for me when I lived in northern British Columbia. Ravens and crows were ubiquitous and highly visible in winter, black forms riding out the storms hunched at the top of spruce trees, or striding across the snow with their curious twine-toed gait, their feathers gleaming as if they had been carved from anthracite, to chisel pieces of discarded hamburger bun from the ice with their ebony beaks. Ravens gave the winter its voice; in the snapping silence of the bush, the ravens would croak and caw, make harsh clicks and crackles, flutings and tender plunkings on a dying minor scale, just like drops of water falling into a pool.

These utterances were sometimes lonely solos, but often two birds will converse, calling and imitating, back and forth. I have engaged crows and ravens in conversation by mimicking the sounds they make. There is a little silence in which you become aware of the bird's bright black eyes watching you and then it will call again, experimentally. Further responses induce more calls, and even if there is no real communication, there is an undeniable frisson of connection despite the language barrier.

The ravens always heralded the arrival of spring. The one sure sign that we might take rising temperatures seriously was the spectacle of a lone black bird flying overhead, carrying a very large twig. From the ground, crows' nests never look as if they require much thought or skill, but they are testaments to the birds' engineering abilities. The higgledy-piggledy pile of branches lodged in the fork of two limbs is just the foundation. On that sturdy layer, the birds construct a saucer of much more tightly woven material. Inside that comes a cup made of down, moss, feathers, grasses, hair—anything soft and cushiony. The whole is an enduring structure; if it is damaged, it does not fall apart, and the birds are capable of effecting repairs and upgrades. The grey jay, a member of the family who lives in the boreal forest, is an even more remarkable architect. For months before it even starts to build a nest in spring, it collects and stores insulating material. It is very hard not to ascribe that to forethought, intelligent planning, and an understanding of the principles of heat loss.

My move south shed new light on these familiar birds for me. I arrived in fall, at a time when all chick-rearing duties were over for the year and the crows had re-formed their giant flocks for a winter of communal living. Standing on the beach late one afternoon in October, I watched one of these flocks making its way to roost on a nearby island. If they had been on foot, I might have described them as strolling home. Unhurried, literally hundreds—probably thousands—of black birds flapped lazily overhead, chattering non-stop. Other bands appeared from different points of the compass, hurrying to catch up with the main procession. It was a massive entity with a single purpose, as sociable and garrulous as a World Cup soccer crowd pouring out of a stadium after a stellar game, reliving the highlights, worrying about finding the car, a few youthful enthusiasts replaying the tackles and redirecting the goals, showing off. Some of the birds frolicked in the air, dodging and weaving, doing barrel rolls and loop-the-loops, their sheer joie de vivre proclaiming their pleasure in flight. They filled the air with their voices and their wingbeats; they took long, long minutes to pass, and still there were stragglers. So vital was their presence that when they had gone, there was an emptiness: the black forms had drained the light from sea and sky; the day was done.

They have an individual presence, too. My father used to tell me about the tame jackdaw (a small crow with a grey head and cape) he had as a boy. I never knew how he had acquired it—maybe it had fallen from the nest or been injured—but from his account it had certainly imprinted on him. He recalled cycling to school with the bird on his shoulder. It would accompany him just so far, and then fly to a particular telegraph pole while he cycled on. When he came back in the afternoon, it would be waiting for him at the same perch; it would fly down as he passed and ride home on his shoulder.

I, too, have briefly enjoyed the trust of an individual bird—a magpie in this case. "One for sorrow," goes the old rhyme about these distinctive black-and-white birds, "Two for joy," but on this occasion the single bird brought nothing but delight.

Alan and I were staying in a tiny house in the village of St. Just in the south of France. We had rented it as a base for a six-week holiday, making daily forays into the countryside to places like Nîmes, Orange, and Avignon as well as countless places of interest well off the tourist track. Our little house was a cool and pleasant place to relax.

It wasn't long after we got there that we noticed a magpie in the surrounding gardens and realized that the people living in the area were familiar with it. I thought I heard one of them calling it Magali, and that is what I called it, too. Magpies are intensely inquisitive; Magali soon found his way to our garden and into our house.

Closer acquaintance revealed the reason for his somewhat unorthodox behaviour. He was very young and must have come a cropper very soon after taking his first flight. His left leg had been injured and he hopped on one foot. His tail feathers were ragged and covered with grey stripes as if they had been abraded by sandpaper. Someone had clipped his wings, though he could manage very short flights. The slightest thing upset his balance, so he spent a lot of time crouched on the ground.

The harsh "Chack, chack" that announced his arrival became very familiar. In spite of his injury, he was extremely agile and quite fearless. He would scramble up and over tables, chairs, and us, prying and stabbing at things with his beak, ripping paper, pulling at shiny objects and hammering anything tough—pencils, books, watch straps, skin.

In no time at all he would rush to greet us when we returned to the house or made an appearance in the morning. He would materialize in doorways and on windowsills, especially when we sat down to eat, march confidently in and help himself to wine from our glasses. He loved peaches and would stuff the skins out of sight under my books, to eat later, I supposed.

One soporific afternoon, when it was really too hot to do anything except sleep, I was pretending to read in the shade outside while I floated on heat and the scent of wild rosemary. Magali clambered up my leg, stabbed in a perfunctory way at my watch and settled on my lap. His beak opened as he panted; I watched the delicate leaf of his tongue, scarlet as arterial blood, flick forward at each breath. I could feel the patter of his heart against my leg. Slowly, his eyelids slid upwards and his head drooped. He was asleep.

We stayed there for three hours, sunk deep in a dreamy lassitude in which nothing existed except us, two living things in wordless accord, suspended in a perfect fusion of warmth and light and well-being. It was a glimpse over the wall of Eden.

Around five o'clock, the declining sun reminded Magali that it was time to eat. He scrambled to the ground and hopped away in search of food. In the days that followed, he was eyeing other magpies as they flew overhead, calling to them. By the time we had to leave, his leg had recovered and he was flying between roofs and treetops.

He had no more time for us. He never slept on my lap again; I am sure he had forgotten us before we left France and that is exactly how it should be.

But I will never forget him. He conferred on me the immense privilege of his trust. For a few fleeting hours I was on terms of perfect equality with a creature quite different from myself. This was not because of anything to do with my status as a human; it was because the bird had allowed me in, accepted me for a little while as a part of his life. The whole experience was wondrously informative—providing insight into the complex nature of a wild bird and an intimate contact that is rarely available—but maybe the most significant revelation was that reversal of roles. It took a decision made by a small, damaged member of a maligned family of birds to show that harmonious co-existence is more than just possible, if humans have the humility to set aside all feelings of superiority and control and accept that our kind is only one among equals: different and powerful, but no more essential than any other.

END RUN

Secretly, they come. One by one, kokanee slip across the sand-bars at the mouth of the creek, their shadows sliding like smoke through the dappled water. More come, and more. They press against the current; they sputter, flailing, through the shallows, harrowing the gravel, writhing in little clouds of sand, squirming and leaping up the tiny rapids where their path narrows round the branches abandoned by the beavers. In the pools, they rest, crowding together, fins fluttering, to gather resolution for the next surge. Mutely, inch by inch, they drive the wide arc of their lives back to its starting point in the magnetic stream.

The secret will out. A heron, a rarity here, flies over the garden from right to left, like a portent. A second follows, rowing unhurriedly, dancer's legs trailing. They make straight for the wood, which borders the creek and which is, now, full of the hidden gossip of birds. The trees croak and caw and bear strange fruits. The branches flex under the scrambling weight of crows and ravens, jostling for position, trading coarse, jolly insults like a cheerful crowd in the bleachers, waiting for the ball game to start. The top of a dead cottonwood suddenly sports a motionless osprey.

The deep pools thicken with the brides and grooms. In the force field of the stream they are all aligned, pointing at the source, drawn to a collective sacrament beneath the eye of a compelling moon. The water is dark, like tea, and at first it is hard to see the sinewy green backs swaying in languid unison. Bending to a viewless wind, they are like hair trailing over the altar stones; they are heavy with sacrifice.

And the wedding guests flock to the ceremony, dressed for a funeral but far from sober. All are uninvited. They elbow each other, clambering over the pews for a better view of the rapt couples, deaf in ritual. Voyeurs, they croak indecent delight, impatient with ceremony and interested only in celebration. Their greedy mouths gape and they calculate the lavishness of the feast with quick, larcenous eyes.

The newlyweds still sway in the dark water, exhausted. Their wedding garments hang ragged now, and they blush. Ghostly rosettes bloom on their sides, stealthy as mildew. Nothing remains for them, and in one after another, the force that keeps them nosing the current drains away, and they surrender to the impulse of the water.

Resolute, they close the circle and lock their deaths with ardour into life. They drift quietly downstream to lay themselves at the feet of the gleaming birds, who lurch across the slick, smooth stones, furiously bickering, to gorge at the raucous, drunken wake.

THE FOX'S TALE

Once upon a time, I knew a fox. Or rather, I knew two foxes, but by a mysterious alchemy, they have become one and the same.

One is a metaphor—the stealthily approaching Thought-Fox from Ted Hughes's poem of the same name, which tracks the evolution of an idea from first glimmer to full expression:

> I imagine this midnight moment's forest:
> Something else is alive
> Beside the clock's loneliness
> And this blank page where my fingers move.

The other was a living animal, barely clinging to existence when I first saw him. As I confront my blank page, ready to tell the tale (which, like any fairy story, even those told in the first person, will be both weighty and weightless), both foxes stir in the forest of *this* midnight moment, of double memory, slipping from tree to tree, noses gently investigating, dogged by blue shadows, neat prints in the snow the only mark of their passage, coming nearer, nearer.

Fox tottered into my life through the gloom of a bitter twilight, one day in late February.

Winter had a stranglehold on the earth that year. Day after day leaden skies pressed down, compacting the snow that had already fallen and promising more. The shrubs in the garden, the line of raspberry canes, even the fence holding the trees at bay were no more than anonymous humps in the landscape. The creek at the edge of our property in Fort St. James had fallen silent months before; silent, too, were the black spruce. Winds had scoured the snow, polishing the surface so that it gleamed in the light from the kitchen window. Every night more flakes drifted down like dust, wearily, as if winter itself were almost exhausted but unable to stop.

That afternoon I had forced myself away from the fire to fill up the bird feeders. Even such a simple chore was an effort. I had five large feeders, and went through many sacks of sunflower seeds in a winter. Clambering up and down steps to reach the containers and hauling them high into the trees on pulleys took time, especially with fingers made exasperatingly wooden by cold. Every expedition across fifty feet of snow to replenish the feeders entailed a double ritual of parka, hat, boots, gloves, as if I were an explorer venturing from my stormbound tent in the Arctic wastes. As I opened the door and let in a chilly fog, I would echo Captain Oates's farewell to his surviving comrades on Scott's ill-conceived Antarctic journey and say to my husband, not quite in jest, "I am just going outside and may be some time."

It was nearly four o'clock and light was draining away fast when I stepped off the deck to flounder across our back garden. In places the crust would support my weight, but in others my leg plunged through to the knee, leaving me lopsided, struggling to stay upright. White clouds hung about my head as I panted with exertion; I could feel the hairs inside my nose stiffen at every breath.

I worked as fast as I could. The chickadees chattered excitedly to one another, their wings purring as they flitted from twig to twig, edging nearer. If I stood still long enough, hands outstretched, they would alight on my fingers and I would feel their feet grip and graze my skin, the quick stab as they snatched a seed from my palm. But it was too cold; my fingers were already stiff and unco-operative and I hurried to finish. As I lumbered back to the waiting house, I threw down some stale bread for the crows. The pieces bounced and slithered on the snow.

A bit later, a casual glance through the kitchen window as I peeled potatoes arrested me. A dark shape was moving about the garden. At first I thought it might be a cat, but it was too big, the legs too long, too thin, the head too angular. Doglike, but not a dog. A fox? But what was he doing?

He moved oddly, lurching a few steps, then dropping his head to the ground. As he moved again, I saw that he was holding one front paw off the ground, hopping awkwardly on the other three. Every so often, the snow crust would collapse treacherously under his weight and he would stumble, instinctively setting down the injured paw to steady himself and snatching it up again. I could almost feel him wince. He was eating the bread I'd thrown out, probably frozen solid by now.

The animal slowly followed an erratic course round the middle of the garden, tracking down every piece of bread. He hunkered down to chew, restlessly turning his head this way and that, and flinching as a raven croaked from the top of a spruce. Finally, he turned and limped away, fading like a wraith into the dark.

Stale bread was no meal for a fox. But it was obvious that the animal had no chance of catching anything; the mice and voles he would normally eat were perfectly safe. Whatever accident had injured his leg, it was likely to be a death sentence. I could see him dragging himself to his den, finally too weak to move, dying alone in the cold, and I hated the thought and my helplessness. But I was not foolish enough to imagine that I could, or should, avert the inevitable. The best I could do—and it was mostly to make *me* feel better—was to put out some more suitable food, just in case the fox returned. All I had was cat biscuits. I shook some onto an aluminum pie plate and left it where the dainty tracks made aimless patterns in the snow. More flakes were drifting down.

"You'd better hurry, Fox," I said out loud, "or they'll be covered up."

I had little faith that the fox would find the biscuits before the squirrels or the crows. An empty plate would tell me only that something had eaten them. Something did. The next morning I found the pie plate overturned; there were no biscuits scattered on the snow. On a hunch, I set the plate out again at about four o'clock; foxes, I thought, might have routes and timetables when they set out to hunt, much like the cat I once knew whose visits to all the households he'd conned into feeding him could be timed to the minute.

I was right. Once again, the fox slipped soundlessly from the trees at dusk and hopped into the open. The light was better, and I could see that he was a cross-fox—a tweedy, grey-brown coat, with black ears. His tail, held straight out, parallel to the ground, seemed at once weighty and weightless, like a club made of gossamer. He gobbled the biscuits in seconds.

So feeding became a routine. One day as I put the plate—rather battered by now—down on the snow, I caught a movement at the edge of my vision. I turned my head very slowly, and there, not five feet away, was the fox. We looked at each other for a moment while I wondered how I could retreat without alarming him. Then I said, "Hello Fox; I'm going now," and started walking backwards to the steps leading up to the deck. He ducked away as I moved, but soon returned to snatch at the biscuits, casting frequent sideways glances at me as I stood near the wall of the house.

"He's getting tame," said my husband, who had been watching from inside.

No, I thought, not that. Desperate, perhaps; ready to ignore the shrilling alarm bells of every instinct that had kept him alive so far in order to eat and exist a little longer. But the fox's need was modifying more than his own behaviour: it was affecting mine, too. Every day that he returned confirmed my response; it wasn't long before I was buying cans of dog food, standing in the pet food aisle reading the nutritional information on each brand, selecting the one with the highest protein content in a bid to return the fox to health as quickly as possible.

Even though Fox was yielding none of his wildness, I hoped, we were becoming intimates. I soon became familiar with his unmistakable smell, a harsh stench that hung about the garden, especially when he took to defecating or urinating on his dish after emptying it—an unappealing habit, but a potent Keep Off signal, nonetheless. His growing tolerance for me brought him closer each day until he stood just two feet away as I spooned the cylinder of pink meat from the can, and gave me the perfect opportunity to inspect him closely.

I could see how emaciated he was. His ribcage and hip bones were starkly visible under the loose drape of lifeless fur, dry and brittle as old straw. His tail was disproportionately large, but close up, no more substantial than thistledown. The black legs looked too thin to support him; three of the feet were elegantly slim but the right front paw dangled, swollen grotesquely, as if he were wearing a single boxing glove. But his eyes were aware and knowing, as if he were barely suppressing a sly amusement, an impression reinforced by his apparent grin as he panted, open-mouthed, tongue flopping, just like a playful dog.

As the days grew infinitesimally longer, drawing into weeks and then months, Fox let down his guard even more. Although still well below freezing, the temperature was rising, so that the snow began to recede from the base of the trees, leaving little wells of dark earth close to the trunks. He often consumed only half of his meal, then picked up the rest, carried it away and dropped it into a tree well, nosing loose snow over his makeshift larder. We were impressed; not only was he able to leave some for later, which suggested that his desperate hunger was a thing of the past, but he was also anticipating a future. Maybe, I thought, fairytale endings *are* sometimes possible.

By the time spring was in the air, and last year's grass, dead as the hair still clinging to a long-buried skull, began to emerge from the snow, Fox was spending a lot of time in our garden. We would come home from work to find him lounging comfortably under a tree, waiting for us. When I started gardening once more, he would fossick about at a safe distance, investigating the turned earth for worms and beetles. On one of these occasions when I was working outside, he managed to astonish me.

I always regarded my garden as a temporary thing. It was no more, really, than an area around the house that had been cleared to create an open space in the nearly eight acres of bush that we called our own. Most of the property remained untouched, except by beavers from the nearby creek, and we liked it that way because it harboured a multitude of animals and birds. The back garden was bordered by a ramshackle fence, purely symbolic in nature, for it kept nothing in or out; it simply marked the edge of the cultivated area. Beyond it the trees massed, the willow and dogwood thickened every year, waiting for the smallest inattention to make their move and reclaim the garden.

So I was kneeling on the ground, diligently weeding a flower bed, when I became aware of a rustling in the bushes beyond the fence. It sounded as if something—more than one something—was running toward me. I was just entertaining the possibility of bears when Fox burst from the undergrowth in full flight, snatching quick glances back over his shoulder. My cat, a diminutive Siamese weighing no more than four pounds, was the next to explode into view, in hot pursuit. They made a wide circle about the lawn, then Fox made straight for me and hid behind my back. The cat screeched to a halt, made an elaborate pretence of unconcern, then walked off, tail twitching. Had that been a hostile attack? Or a game? By the time I looked round, Fox had gone.

And then it hit me. Fox had been *running*. On *four feet.*

As if this had been a farewell demonstration, Fox dropped out of sight. He stopped coming for food. We missed him, but were happy that he no longer needed us. Sometimes I would lie in bed listening to a fox's staccato bark tearing the darkness and savour the distant link to his busy secret life, grateful for the evidence of his continued well-being. I could not imagine a more satisfactory end to the story.

But there was more.

One evening Fox appeared in the garden again. I had long since removed his battered plate, but I hurtled downstairs to fetch one of the remaining cans of dog food, and rushed up again to open it before he left, yelling to my bemused husband, "Fox is back!" Fox made short work of half the meat, picked up the rest and hid it under his usual tree, then trotted out of sight.

Half an hour later I caught sight of him again, crossing the road and ducking beneath the fence in the front of the house. He was not alone. A slightly smaller, darker fox ran with him. They went straight to Fox's larder and, after they had both rooted about a bit, Fox stood back to allow his companion to eat.

Nor was that the end. Late one afternoon in early summer, when the air was heavy with the scent of wild roses, something unusual about the view ahead caught my wandering attention on the drive home from school. Just opposite my house, on the other side of the road, there was a trail leading into the woods and swamps that bordered Stuart Lake. Right where that trail met the roadway stood Fox. His mate lay beside him and four cubs tumbled over and around her. Watching them from a distance, until Fox abruptly turned away from the road and led his family down the trail, to disappear one by one into the green shade of towering poplars, gave me a moment of the purest joy I have ever experienced.

And they lived happily ever after. So the fairy tales always end. Reason and experience make us smile wryly at the phrase, but sometimes, very occasionally, it is no less than the truth. Fox and Thought-Fox meld in the shadows and slip across the snow-covered garden, the details of ear and eye and will to live sharper and more defined with each paw print, until the "sudden sharp hot stink" announces his arrival in "the dark hole of the head," and Fox steps fully realized, breathing, forever warm, onto the page.

COMPANIONS AFLOAT

 The ark sails on, but the *baiji* has disappeared from the passenger list.

I had clicked on the Science/Nature section of the online BBC International News, and there it was. Reporting on a six-week-long visual and acoustic survey undertaken in November and December 2006, a team of scientists concluded that the baiji, a rare freshwater dolphin found only in the Yangtze River, is now "likely to be extinct."

I imagine the scientists on their two boats, tirelessly scanning the murky waters of the great river with binoculars and sonar, hoping for a glimpse of the white bodies, a sign that the long narrow beaks were still snapping up fish, an echo of their calls, a blip on the screens that might indicate the presence of a large mammal. Six long weeks in the creature's only habitat and they saw and heard nothing. The dolphin had already appeared as "critically endangered" on the World Conservation Union's Red List of Threatened Species. So no surprise, perhaps, but still Dr. Sam Turvey refers to the findings as a "shocking tragedy."

And tragedy it is. The baiji was the only remaining member of the Lipotidae, an ancient family that separated from all other marine mammal species around forty to twenty million years ago. That it has disappeared from the face of the Earth after so long—an infinitely longer presence than our own—is sad enough, but the reasons for its extinction should make us hang our heads.

Nobody set out to exterminate the baijis. The researchers concluded that there were several contributory factors in the creature's demise: the construction of the Three Gorges Dam; collisions with boats on the crowded Yangtze; uncontrolled pollution of the water; and relentless attrition as by-catch in unregulated local fishing, "which used rolling hooks, nets and electrofishing." In other words, the baiji was collateral damage, the unintended victim of massive human impact on its environment. In a few short years, human activity mangled, bludgeoned, poisoned, gouged, drowned, electrocuted, and crowded them out of existence.

Any death chills the blood of the living. The death of a species has its own ominous resonance; the picking off, one by one, of so many living organisms ignites nightmarish possibilities in the mind of the one creature (as far as we know) with the imagination and foresight to contemplate its own mortality. When it is our fault, what are we to think?

The baiji is an extreme example, but there are plenty of other animals in desperate straits. The World Conservation Union documents their conservation status on its Red List. Currently there are 844 extinctions: 784 documented extinctions and sixty species classed as extinct in the wild, but surviving in captivity. This number is slowly rising, which is bad enough, but of far greater concern are the ones entering the endangered or critically endangered categories. In 2008, the Canadian government added thirty-six names to the list of animals and plants protected under the Species At Risk Act. Nearly all of them are clinging to existence in isolated, increasingly fragmented habitats, threatened by human encroachment and the inevitable consequences of their own isolation and diminishing genetic diversity. The words that recur over and over in the descriptions of each species tell the story: habitat degradation; erosion; drainage; encroachment; logging practices; invasion of non-native plants and animals; over-grazing; predation.

The headlong, heedless smash and grab of human progress has produced so many inadvertent victims that it is probably beyond us to embrace and rescue them all. It is hard enough to protect the conservation superstars—the great apes, the pandas, the whales, the tigers—and next to impossible to generate enough enthusiasm for all the threatened amphibians and corals and lichens. Who will adopt the Ord's Kangaroo Rat as a mascot? Who will cherish the Blue-grey Taildropper slug? (The name alone would be worth fighting for.) In fact, most ordinary people, contemplating such a Herculean task, probably share the very same helplessness I remember as a small child when I severed an earthworm.

I was digging with a trowel, trying to prepare my own little patch of garden for the flower seeds that my father had brought home for me. It was hard work in that London clay. Even though I gripped the handle with both hands, the tool twisted awkwardly in the resistant soil. To make it pierce the crust and slice deep, I had to throw my whole weight upon it.

There was a sudden yielding and, triumphantly, I levered up the trowelful of earth and dumped it out beside the hole. Something was moving in the crumbled soil. Half an earthworm writhed from side to side, blindly. At the bottom of the hole, the other half of the animal stirred feebly. I was appalled.

Carefully, trying very hard not to squeeze it, I lifted the segment from the hole, set the severed ends together as close as possible, and watched, as if some magical weld might reunite the halves. What I thought of as the front end was still squirming, mutely demanding action.

I ran indoors to find an empty box and to rummage in my mother's sewing basket. Outside again, I filled the matchbox with earth so that the worm would feel at home, then put the piece of narrow pink satin ribbon flat on the ground and laid the severed ends across it. I was not at all sure I had got the two parts the right way up—suppose its head was now facing the wrong way?—but that was the least of my problems. It was very difficult to keep the cut ends together at all as I wrapped the ribbon around the stricken creature, and the wounds made the bandage wet and sticky, but I persevered and managed to tie a bow at last. (I once had a bridesmaid's dress with bows like that all the way down the front.) I put the patient in the matchbox and slid the lid closed so that it would be dark, the way worms prefer it, and left it to rest.

When I peeked at it later, because I had to, both halves of the worm were still and leathery. The front half had discarded the bandage; the ribbon was filthy. I buried the whole lot in the hole, but the lessons of inattention, of misdirected sentiment and futile atonement would not go away. Guilt and remorse have a very long half-life.

While there is a natural extinction rate that has seen 99 per cent of all species which have ever existed disappear, scientists now believe that human activity is accelerating that rate by up to ten thousand times. This is on a par with the cataclysmic event 65 million years ago that caused the extinction of the dinosaurs. Richard Leakey has called the modern version "the Sixth Mass Extinction." And unlike the previous five, it is entirely man-made.

Belatedly as usual, humankind—or at least, some portion of it—is becoming aware. We have a World Wildlife Fund; we have Greenpeace; we have the Sierra Club. There are prophets sounding the alarm: Rachel Carson, Davids Suzuki and Attenborough, Jane Goodall, to name just a few. We list endangered species, and in response, zoos and research facilities undertake breeding programs, poachers are prosecuted (when they can be caught), sanctuaries and vast preserves are created, trade in certain animal parts is proscribed, we mount Save the Whale and Save the Spotted Owl campaigns, we even talk of DNA banks and cloning—anything to ensure that our children and grandchildren may be able to see a living Siberian tiger or northern white rhino for themselves. Though they'd better be quick with the rhinoceros; there are only nineteen northern whites left in the world.

There are glimmers of hope. In the same year the baiji disappeared, the Attenborough's long-beaked echidna, feared extinct, reappeared in Papua New Guinea, if the holes found, characteristic of the ones they poke in the ground in their search for worms, were anything to go by. Villagers claimed not only to have seen echidnas, but also to have eaten them!

In Britain, the European Union policy of paying farmers to take fields out of production in order to reduce the infamous "food mountains" led to the restoration of the woodlark's habitat, and a resurgence of this critically endangered bird from a low point of 241 breeding pairs in 1986 to 3,084 pairs in 2007.

An expedition into an area of the war torn Congo just west of Lake Tanganyika, off limits to scientists for more than fifty years, revealed that a thousand square kilometres of forest, stretching from the lakeshore to 2,725 metres above sea level, remain intact. In two months, the expedition members discovered six animal species unknown to science, as well as a number of unidentifiable plant species, in an area teeming with more familiar wildlife.

"If we can find six new species in such a short period, it makes you wonder what else is out there," commented Wildlife Conservation Society researcher Andrew Plumptre.

Yes, indeed. Humans have catalogued only 1,8,000,000 species worldwide, a mere 10 per cent of the life forms on Earth. What of that unknown 90 per cent, those millions of invisible passengers on the ark? How many of them do we blindly crush and starve, dispossess and poison? How many of them are like the humble leopard frog, which scientists now think might be valuable in treating certain kinds of brain tumours? Or like the so-called hemorrhage plant, *Aspilia africana*, long used in African traditional medicine, whose leaves can stop bleeding, block infection, and speed healing?

In the past fifty years, conservation and ecology have increased their grip on the public imagination. More and more, green is the favourite colour. But knowing is not enough; remorse is not enough; band-aid remedies are not enough.

Awareness has to take a further step. Those people who have sounded alarms and pioneered the way back to a healthier planet—from the household names like Rachel Carson, Jane Goodall, David Suzuki, Alexandra Morton and Al Gore, through members of organizations such as the Sierra Club and Greenpeace, and all the way to those anonymous individuals who rehabilitate injured animals, donate money to supply water to Third World villages, and toil at organic farming—have internalized a basic truth which is no less valuable for being obvious to all who are prepared to understand. "Seldom if ever," says Rachel Carson in *Silent Spring*, "does Nature operate in closed and separate compartments." In the balanced world that nature produced over hundreds of millions of years, everything had its place and nothing dominated to the disadvantage of anything else. The environment moulded all the special adaptations. Where there were harmful effects, time—vast quantities of time—healed them. These were the rules of existence until mankind found the power in the twentieth century to turn the whole equation on its head. In a tearing hurry, humans made life modify its surroundings, and now there is hardly time enough to put it right.

There are signs that the philosophical tide has turned. The wider view, of the infinitely complex web of connections, of the checks and balances between all living organisms, offers the key to making some kind of start at buying time for nature to restore the equilibrium we have upset.

This movement is apparent in the current work of Jane Goodall, who decided one day, after a lifetime of observing and teaching people about the chimpanzee, that she could no longer sit in her beautiful forest in Tanzania and instead, set about forming partnerships with small groups of people on projects that restore farmland, encourage useful crops, and teach sustainable farming methods that thrive in the environment rather than pervert it. She has now expressed cautious optimism about the future: because of nature's amazing resilience and because of "the indomitable human spirit; people won't give up." Only time will tell if her confidence in individual effort and collective will is justified. In the meantime, there is work to do.

The ark that is the Earth sails on through cosmic seas, taking on a little water, the bilge pumps wheezing ominously. On such a lengthy cruise, surely it is natural to surrender to the vessel's pace: why choose such a mode of transport if the object is to arrive quickly? Almost every passenger quietly takes each day as it comes, those on the day shift yawning and stretching in the chilly dawn as they make room for the night creatures to burrow into the warm gloom below decks. Only the humans stand at the bow at all hours, complaining about the food and the incompetent navigation, willing the ship to go faster, peering and peering at the far horizon, longing for a glimpse of land, even though they have never seen their destination and cannot know if they will like it when they arrive.

It is time for humans to stop behaving like the First Class passengers on the *Titanic*, consuming every luxury, oblivious to the Third Class battened below hatches in the holds. We can make a start by doing what everybody does in the enforced intimacy of a cruise ship: get to know our fellow passengers. We can begin with the nearest—the Dalmatian sitting beside us at dinner, the Siamese cat occupying the next deck chair, the family of rabbits in the opposite cabin. We can ask where they live, what they do, and listen to their stories, even learn their secrets. We can become attuned to shipboard life, learn the diplomacy and compromise of a closed world, take our turn on the bucket brigade when the bilge pumps fail.

We had better do this because our fellow passengers, down to the very humblest plankton and lichen, have always had the right idea about life and could teach us a thing or two about co-existence. We had better do this because, relying solely on our own impaired judgment and self-interest, we've made such a mess of the world. We had better do this because if we don't, our only defence against our children's accusing eyes will echo my long-ago lament as I hid the murdered worm: "But I didn't mean to do it!" And how could such a feeble excuse for an excuse appease those children, survive their withering condemnation, if they are never able to wander, enraptured, as I once did, through Eden?

MARGARET THOMPSON's first collection of short stories, *Hide and Seek*, was published in 1996, and in 2000, she won a BC2000 Book Award for her second book, a historical novel for young adults, *Eyewitness*. She has published stories, poems, and essays in literary magazines and anthologies, as well as a chapter book called *Fox Winter* and a collection of travel essays, *Knocking on the Moonlit Door*. A past president of the Federation of BC Writers, Margaret sits on the editorial board of the Federation's quarterly journal, *WordWorks*. Born in England and educated at London University, Exeter University, and San Diego State University, Margaret has taught in the BC towns of Merritt, Madeira Park, Sechelt, and Fort St. James. She now lives in Victoria, BC, where she is able to pursue one of her favourite occupations, birdwatching.